TABLE OF CONTENTS

ACRONYMS ii

ILLUSTRATIONS vi

INTRODUCTION 1

    Methodology 6

U.S. WAR PLANNING 8

    The Colored War Plans 11
    Rainbow War Plans 16

OAHU DEFENSE PLAN 21

PRE-WAR U.S. INTELLIGENCE COMMUNITY 33

    Intelligence Groups in Hawaii 34
    Navy Intelligence Organizations 35
    Army Intelligence Organizations 36
    Federal Bureau of Investigation 37
    State Department 39
    Office of the Coordination of Information 41
    Sources of Information and Intelligence 41

WAKING THE SLEEPING GIANT - THE ATTACK ON PEARL HARBOR 48

CONCLUSION 53

    Findings 53
    Implications 57

BIBLIOGRAPHY 60

ACRONYMS

ACW	Aircraft Control and Warning
AIC	Army Air Corps
AWS	Army Warning Service
CIA	Central Intelligence Agency
CINCLANT	Commander in Chief, Atlantic Command
CINCPAC	Commander in Chief, Pacific Fleet
CINCUS	Commander in Chief U.S. Fleet
CNO	Chief of Naval Operations
COI	Office of the Coordination of Information
COM-14	14th Naval District
DHS	Department of Homeland Security
DIO	Navy District Intelligence Office
FBI	Federal Bureau of Investigation
G-2	Army Intelligence Division
G-5	Army War Plans Division
IJN	Imperial Japanese Navy
JCFDP	Joint Coastal Frontier Defense Plan
J-Series	American Term for group of Japanese code
J-19	American term for Tsu code; code was assigned to Japan's Honolulu consulate for its radio communication with Japan
MAGIC	American term for all Japanese diplomatic codes and cipher
MI-8	Military Intelligence, Section 8- Signals Intelligence
MID	U.S. Army Military Intelligence Division
ONI	Office of Naval Intelligence
OP-16	Office of Naval Intelligence
OP-20	Office of Naval Communication

OPNAV   Office of Naval Operations

Orange   U.S. code term for Japan

PURPLE   American term for the top priority Japanese diplomatic cipher

SIS   Signal Intelligence Service

Military Rank Structure – Army Grade/Rank

Pay Grade	Abbreviation	Title
W-1	WO1	Warrant Officer
CW-2	CWO2	Chief Warrant Officer 2
CW-3	CWO3	Chief Warrant Officer 3
CW-4	CWO4	Chief Warrant Officer 4
CW-5	CWO5	Chief Warrant Officer 5
O-1	2LT	Second Lieutenant
O-2	1LT	First Lieutenant
O-3	CPT	Captain
O-4	MAJ	Major
O-5	LTC	Lieutenant Colonel
O-6	COL	Colonel
O-7	BG	Brigadier General
O-8	MG	Major General
O-9	LTG	Lieutenant General
O-10	GEN	General
Special	GA	General of the Army

Military Rank Structure – Navy Grade/Rank

W-1	WO1	Warrant Officer (No longer in use)
CW-2	CWO2	Chief Warrant Officer 2
CW-3	CW03	Chief Warrant Officer 3
CW-4	CWO4	Chief Warrant Officer 4
CW-5	CWO5	Chief Warrant Officer 5
O-1	ENS	Ensign
O-2	LTJG	Lieutenant Junior Grande
O-3	LT	Lieutenant
O-4	Lt. Comdr.	Lieutenant Commander
O-5	Comdr.	Commander
O-6	CAPT	Captain
O-7	Rear Adm.	Rear Admiral (Lower Half)
O-8	RADM	Rear Admiral (Upper Half)
O-9	ADM	Vice Admiral
O-10	ADM	Admiral Chief of Naval Operations/ Commandant CG
O-10	FADM	Fleet Admiral (Special

.

ILLUSTRATIONS

Page

Figure 1. Rainbow War Plans..21

Figure 2. Pacific Fleet Organization..24

Figure 3. Army and Navy Intelligence Structure and Communication Sharing Channels.............37

DUE TO COPYRIGHT RESTRICTIONS
SOME OR ALL IMAGES ARE NOT INCLUDED

INTRODUCTION

Increasingly strained diplomatic relations between Japan and the United States

throughout the first decades of the twentieth century culminated in the Japanese attack against

Pearl Harbor on December 7, 1941. Japan and the United States had enjoyed mutually beneficial

diplomatic and trade relations for decades, but tensions started to mount in the early 1930s.

President Theodore Roosevelt brokered in 1905 the peace treaty that concluded the Russo-

Japanese War, with terms that favored Japan.[1] The United States and Japan maintained a good

diplomatic relationship for several more years, illustrated by their Commerce and Navigation

Treaty of 1911– a vital treaty for Japan given its severe lack of natural resources, including

strategic materials such as ores and petroleum to supply its military and other industries. Between

1911 and 1939, the United States remained Japan's major supplier of such material. However,

during this time Japan also embarked on a path toward economic independence, doing so by

seeking to create an empire similar to that of the British.[2]

To reduce its dependence on other countries for natural resources, Japan initiated in the

1890's a series of measures to attain economic control of the Asia-Pacific region.[3] Because of

Japan's increasingly aggressive foreign policy, President Roosevelt instructed the Army War

---

[1]Jeffrey J. Gudmens, *Staff Ride Handbook for the Attack on Pearl Harbor, 7 December 1941: A Study of Defending America* (Fort Leavenworth: Combat Studies Institute Press, 1960), 48; Ian W. Toll, *Pacific Crucible: War at Sea in the Pacific, 1941-1942* (New York: W.W. Norton & Company, 2012), xxviii.

[2]Gordon W. Prange, *At Dawn We Slept: The Untold Story of Pearl Harbor* (New York: Penguin Books Ltd., 1981), 5; United States Army Center of Military History, *A Brief History of the U.S. Army in World War II* (Washington D.C.: Government Printing Office, 1992), 31; Toll, 234.

[3]George C. Herring, *From Colony to Superpower: U.S. Foreign Relations Since 1776* (Oxford: Oxford University Press, 2008), 530; Gudmens, *Staff Ride Handbook*, 41; Encyclopedia Britannica Online, s. v. "Sino-Japanese War," accessed January 12, 2013, http://www.britannica.com/EBchecked/topic/546176/Sino-Japanese-War.

College in 1907 to, in historian Harry P. Ball's words, "Prepare plans based on the assumption of a war with Japan. This was the beginning of Army planning participation in "Plan Orange" for war with Japan, a plan that would keep more than a generation of planners employed." For the next few decades, Army War College classes acted as an extension of the War Department's War Plans Division, analyzing, war gaming, and recommending changes to actual war plans maintained by the War Department.[4]

By 1931, diplomatic and economic relations between the United States and Japan began to sour. The government of Japan could not cope with the burdens of the global Great Depression, which soon led to its replacement by a militarist government. The new regime took steps to improve Japan's economic situation by forcibly annexing resource-rich areas in the Asia-Pacific, focusing first on China.[5] It began this process by ordering the Japanese Army to invade Manchuria. The army quickly conquered the Chinese province, and the Japanese government announced that it had annexed Manchuria, renaming it "Manchukuo."[6]

The United States refused to acknowledge the Japanese annexation of Manchuria, but did not plan or threaten any military or economic retaliation because American business and political leaders did not want to disrupt lucrative trade arrangements with Japan.[7] In addition to a variety of consumer goods, Japan purchased most of its scrap iron and steel from the United States. Most

[4]Harry P. Ball, *Of Responsible Command: A History of the U.S. Army War College* (Carlisle Barracks: Alumni Association of the United States Army, 1994), 109-10.

[5]Herring, *From Colony to Superpower*, 530; Gudmens, *Staff Ride Handbook*, 49.

[6]Sandra Wilson, *The Manchurian Crisis and Japanese Society*, 1931-33 (London: Routledge, 2002), 16; William B. Hopkins, *The Pacific War: The Strategy, Politics, and Players That Won The War* (Minneapolis: Zenith Press, 2008), 15.

[7]Herring, *From Colony to Superpower,* 489.

importantly, Japan bought 80 percent of its oil from America.[8] American government officials did speak out against this act of aggression, but Japan ignored their protests, and in the summer of 1937 launched a full-scale attack on the rest of China. Although this continuation of Japanese expansionism concerned U.S. government leaders, President Franklin D. Roosevelt remained true to America's longstanding isolationist policy and again refused to respond militarily to stop Japanese expansion.[9]

The United States did not take action until 1939 to contest the continued Japanese aggression in China. That year the United States announced its withdrawal from the 1911 Treaty of Commerce and Navigation, indicating an end to trade with Japan.[10] Nevertheless, Japan continued its military campaign in China, so in 1940 Roosevelt declared the additional step of imposing a partial embargo of U.S. shipments of oil, gasoline, and metals to Japan. This merely led Japan to look elsewhere to procure resources – primarily French Indochina.[11] The Japanese also considered the Dutch East Indies as a possible source for oil; however, this option included significant military risk since America controlled the Philippines with a sizable land force, and its Pacific Fleet, based at Pearl Harbor, Hawaii, controlled the waters between Japan and the Dutch East Indies.[12]

---

[8]Hopkins, *The Pacific War*, 35; Toll, *Pacific Crucible*, 116; Jeffery Record, "Japan's Decision for War in 1941: Some Enduring Lessons" (master's thesis, U.S. Army War College, 2009), 15; Frank Vandiver, *1001 Things Everyone Should Know About World War II* (New York: Random House Inc., 2002), 7.

[9]Allan R. Millet and Peter Maslowski, *For the Common Defense A Military History of the United States of America* (New York: The Free Press, 1994), 414.

[10]Justus D. Doenecke and John E. Wilz, *From Isolation to War, 1931 – 1941* (Arlington Heights: Harlan Davidson, Inc., 1991), 120-21.

[11]Herring, *From Colony to Superpower*, 486; Roberta Wohlstetter, *Pearl Harbor Warning and Decision* (Stanford: Stanford University Press, 1962), 77.

[12]John Keegan, *Intelligence in War: The Value and Limitations of What the Military Can*

America's 1940 embargo failed to achieve the desired results, so in July 1941 the United States government imposed a comprehensive embargo on outside resources headed to Japan and froze all Japanese assets in America.[13] This action placed Japan in an untenable economic position that left the country's leaders convinced that only a military response could break the logjam. With the approval of Japanese Emperor Hirohito, the Japanese Navy began planning for attacks on Pearl Harbor, the Philippines, and other bases in the Pacific in early December that might enable them to open a route to the Dutch East Indies.[14] The Japanese focused on the U.S. Pacific Fleet at Pearl Harbor because no other force in the Pacific could pose a significant challenge to the Japanese Navy. Furthermore, the Philippines would pose a threat to Japan's lines of communication as long as America controlled the bases there, since every oil tanker heading from the south Pacific to Japan would have to pass by American-held Luzon. These factors remained central to Japanese strategy as it developed war plans.[15]

Thus, the Japanese attack on Pearl Harbor served as part of a grand strategy of conquest in the western Pacific. Japan's military planners sought to immobilize the U.S. Pacific Fleet so that the United States could not interfere with Japanese plans to invade and seize control of resource-rich territory in the Pacific. A sneak attack against the bulk of the U.S. fleet seemed the most logical and effective means to achieve this objective. Alfred T. Mahan, an American naval officer and strategist, developed naval doctrine in which he emphasized the offensive naval battle.

Learn About the Enemy (New York: Vintage Books, 2002), 189 – 190; Center of Military History, *A Brief History of the U.S. Army in World War II*, 31.

[13]Toll, *Pacific Crucible*, 116; Herring, *From Colony to Superpower*, 531, 534; Hans L. Trefousse, *What Happened at Pearl Harbor? Documents Pertaining to Japanese Attack of December 7, 1941, and Its Background* (New York: Twayne Publishers, 1958), 15.

[14]Robert B. Stinnett, *Day of Deceit: The Truth about FDR and Pearl Harbor* (New York: The Free Press, 2000), 30.

[15]Center of Military History, *A Brief History of the U.S. Army in World War II*, 31-32.

As historian Ian Toll has written, Alfred T. Mahan's theory of the "decisive battle had a deep and lasting impression in Japan."[16] The Japanese Naval Staff College attempted unsuccessfully to recruit Mahan to join its faculty. Nevertheless, the Japanese military adopted Mahan's doctrine of the decisive battle at both the Japanese navy and army colleges.[17] As a result, the Imperial Japanese Navy (IJN) believed that victory against the United States relied on victory in a decisive naval battle; this would allow the Japanese to command the sea, thereby avoiding a protracted war with the United States.[18]

In time, Japan would also have to seize America's central Pacific bases at Guam and the Wake islands and invade the Philippines to make its overall strategy work. By crippling American naval power in the Pacific, Japan's military leaders believed they could freely seize Burma, Malaya, Singapore, and the Dutch East Indies in a series of rapid amphibious operations. With these resource-rich locations under its control, Japan could then shift to a defensive strategy by establishing a ring of fortified islands around the newly seized territory in the south and the central Pacific. Finally, Japan's leaders anticipated little resistance from the Americans who, once involved in the European war, would lack the will or military power to fight on a second front in the Pacific, leading them to settle for a negotiated peace.[19]

---

[16]Toll, *Pacific Crucible*, xvi-xix; Steven M. Gillion, *FDR Leads The Nation Into War* (New York: Basic Books, 2011), 44; Alan D. Zimm, *Attack On Pearl Harbor: Strategy, Combat, Myths, Deceptions* (Havertown: Casemate Publishers, 2011), 371; Hopkins, *The Pacific War*, 33-34.

[17]Hopkins, *The Pacific War*, xix.

[18]Gillion, *FDR Leads The Nation Into* War, 44; Zimm, *Attack On Pearl Harbor*, 371; Toll, *Pacific Crucible*, xvi-xix, 120; Hopkins, *The Pacific War,* 33-34; Record, "Japan's Decision for War in 1941," 21-24, 33. The Japanese Navy successfully utilized Mahan's naval theory during the Russo-Japanese War, giving them faith in its effectiveness.

[19]Keegan, *Intelligence in War*, 189; Kent Roberts Greenfield, ed. *The War Against Japan, U.S. Army in World War II Pictorial Record* (Washington D.C.: Government Printing Office, 2001), 2.

Throughout this period of intense military planning, the Japanese kept diplomatic lines open with the United States in the hope that an opportunity might emerge to negotiate an end to the embargo. Any such hope vanished on November 26, 1941 when U.S. Secretary of State Cordell Hull handed the Japanese ambassadors in Washington D.C. what historians now refer to as the Hull Note.[20] The note listed three prerequisites for any relief from the U.S. resource embargo: removal of all troops from China, removal of all troops from Indochina, and an end to the alliance Japan had signed with Germany and Italy the previous year.[21] Japan would not accept these conditions, and in many historians' estimation, could not thrive as a nation under the economic constraints the United States would impose upon it even if it did. Regardless, by the time Secretary of State Hull delivered this note to the Japanese diplomats, the Imperial Navy was already sailing for Hawaii and the Philippines. World War II in the Pacific was only days away.[22]

Methodology

Many historians of World War II have asserted that the U.S. Army did not effectively plan or prepare for an attack on Pearl Harbor by the Japanese Navy, and this increased the severity of the losses suffered by American forces during the attack.[23] However, not all historians

---

[20]Henry C. Clausen and Bruce Lee, *Pearl Harbor: Final Judgment* (New York: Crown Publishers, Inc., 1992), 2.

[21]Stinnett, *Day of Deceit*, 218; Evan Mawdsley, *Countdown to Global War, Part Three* (New Haven: Yale Books, 2008), http://www.yalebooks. wordpress.com (accessed 26 November 2011); Toll, *Pacific Crucible*, 122; Wohlstetter, *Pearl Harbor*, 263.

[22]Wohlstetter, *Pearl Harbor*, 263-77.

[23]Zimm, *Attack On Pearl Harbor*, 218; Henry G. Gole, *The Road to Rainbow: Army Planning for Global War, 1934-1940* (Annapolis: Naval Institute Press, 2003), 153; Wohlstetter, *Pearl Harbor*, 23-25; Richard Freeman, *Pearl Harbor: Hinge of War* (Chicago: University of Chicago Press, 2007), 341. Gole wrote that Japan's attack on Pearl Harbor was an operational surprise. Wohlstetter argued that the Hawaiian Department had not exercised its plans to ensure its readiness to defend the island of Oahu, and that the organizations identified in the defense plans lacked the personnel and equipment to execute them. Similarly, Freeman wrote that Oahu lacked the equipment to defend the island, regardless of the amount of planning and preparation

have lauded the success of the Japanese attack, pointing out how quickly the U.S. Navy recovered from the damage it suffered, and many historians have argued that the Army prepared reasonably well for an attack and conducted the best defense possible given the Army's size, budget, and the quality and quantity of its equipment in 1941.[24] This leads to the still-debated question whether the Japanese Navy's success on December 7, 1941 resulted primarily from a lack of American planning for such an attack, poor early warning systems and procedures, or an ineffective response. Revisiting the historical debate regarding the cause of Japan's success in its 1941 attack against Pearl Harbor offers insight for today's homeland defense planners hoping to prevent another attack on U.S. soil like the one conducted by Al Qaeda on September 11, 2001, as parallels to recent events in America will demonstrate.

A historical review of three major factors: war planning; intelligence gathering; and the information sharing, early warning, and collective response methods utilized by U.S. organizations stationed at Pearl Harbor will enable the identification of specific U.S. shortcomings both in the lead-up to the attack and in the actions taken on the day of the attack. Comparing the relative significance of these shortcomings against these evaluation criteria will enable identification of the primary cause of the success that the Japanese achieved. These evaluation criteria roughly correspond to three periods of history: the U.S. interwar period, the

that took place.

[24]Prange and Goldstein, *At Dawn We Slept*, 549-50, 737; Toll, *Pacific Crucible*, 159-60; Senate Joint Committee, *Report on the Investigation of the Pearl Harbor Attack*, 79th Cong., 2nd sess., 1946, Executive Summary, 76-77, 82. Some historians assert that the after the initial shock of the attack wore off, American officials realized that the attack on Pearl Harbor was not devastating. For example, some historians have pointed out that the Japanese merely destroyed old naval vessels, because the Five Power Treaty that the United States signed with Japan left the United States with minimal vessel tonnage and an aged fleet. The attack prompted the U.S. Navy to build a modern fleet with the aircraft carrier at its core. This led the Secretary of War to write in February 1941 to the Secretary of the Navy that he believed that the Pacific Fleet in Hawaii as rebuilt after Pearl Harbor stood out as the best equipped of all of the overseas departments' naval forces.

beginning of hostilities in Europe through the attack at Pearl Harbor, and the actual attack at Pearl Harbor.

As early as 1898, the United States understood the strategic importance of the Hawaiian Islands to its security in the Pacific and began planning to counter any possible aggression from Japan.[25] The War Department continually refined its plans throughout the decades preceding the beginning of World War II, and committed resources to the Hawaiian Department to implement the plans in accordance with national security priorities and within the means available to the U.S. Army. As the following analysis demonstrates, U.S. intelligence services anticipated and planned for an attack against Pearl Harbor, and the Hawaiian Department prepared diligently to defend itself in the event of such an attack. The success of the Japanese attack did not result from poor intelligence preparation or defense planning. Rather, the degree of success the Japanese achieved resulted primarily from the lack of an effective early warning system and the resulting inability to respond to the indications and warnings detected by Hawaiian Department-based intelligence personnel that anticipated and later detected the imminent attack. The inability to fuse the intelligence available in the days and hours leading up to the Japanese attack led to poor early warning, but ultimately the Hawaiian Department's inability to respond rapidly and effectively to the attack, however early Army or Navy personnel detected its approach, served as America's Achilles Heel. Given the logical limits of its capability, U.S. forces simply could not assemble and mount a defense quickly enough to fend off a determined attack at this point in America's military development.

U.S. WAR PLANNING

Notwithstanding the fact that Japan and the United States fought together as allies during

---

[25]Edward S. Miller, *War Plan Orange: The U.S. Strategy to Defeat Japan, 1879-1945* (Annapolis: Naval Institute Press, 1991), 44.

World War I, American war planners focused during the interwar period on the possibility of war with Japan.[26] Although the United States adopted an isolationist mentality after World War I, it recognized the deteriorating relationship with Japan. As historian Edward S. Miller has written, ". . . the root cause would be Japan's quest for national greatness by attempting to dominate the land, people, and resources of the Far East."[27] The United States viewed itself as the protectorate of Western influence in the region and favored open international trade. Therefore, Japan could only achieve its expansionist goals in the Pacific if it removed American influence from the region – a fact both countries recognized. Japan intended to achieve this by denying the United States access to bases in the Philippines, Guam, and the Hawaiian Islands. The 1907 war scare with Japan led to the initiation in America of war planning against the threat of Japanese aggression, and the establishment of a standing American planning capability at the Army War College.[28]

Tension between the two countries escalated in 1907 when the United States passed a series of laws aimed at Japanese immigrants, including school segregation and restrictive property rights laws.[29] The government of Japan believed these laws violated treaties signed by both countries. The Roosevelt administration attempted to decrease tensions by negotiating a gentlemen's agreement with the Japanese government in which Japan would reduce the flow of immigration, but this only decreased tension in the short term.[30] In the summer of that year, President Roosevelt instructed the Army War College to prepare plans based upon the

---

[26]Gudmens, *Staff Ride Handbook*, 38.

[27]Miller, *War Plan Orange*, 3.

[28]Ball, *Of Responsible Command*, 109.

[29]Ian W. Toll, *Pacific Crucible*, xxix.

[30]Miller, *War Plan Orange*, 21.

contingency of a war with Japan. On June 12 the War College faculty integrated "Problem Number 12" into the curriculum to comply with the Chief of Staff's instructions: this problem involved measures taken to meet a sudden attack by Japan under existing conditions. The Army and Navy Joint Board developed and endorsed a preliminary plan and two days later, on 27 June, the board presented the plan to the President. As historian Harry P. Ball states "Problem No. 12 was the beginning of Army planning participation in Plan Orange for war with Japan, a plan that would keep more than a generation of planners employed."[31]

Since 1903 the Joint Army and Navy Board had overseen America's strategic war planning.[32] From its inception through the end of World War I, the Board consistently proved ineffectual, producing plans of little strategic value. This led to the Board's reorganization in 1919 to one headed by six powerful members: the Army Chief of Staff and the heads of the War Department's Operations and War Plans divisions, the Chief of Naval Operations (CNO), the Assistant CNO, and the senior naval war planning officer.[33] . The board also operated under a new charter, giving it the authority to initiate studies that it deemed necessary rather than waiting for a request from a cabinet secretary. Adding to its efficacy, the members had a close but informal relationship. In addition, the Joint Board had its own dedicated staff, the Joint Planning Committee (JPC), composed of six mid-level officers, three each from the Army and Navy War Plans Divisions.[34]

---

[31]Ball, *Of Responsible Command*, xxxi.

[32]Brian M. Linn, *Guardians of Empire, The U.S. Army and the Pacific, 1902-1940* (Chapel Hill: University of North Carolina Press, 1997), 54.

[33]Ball, *Of Responsible Command*, 174.

[34]Miller, *War Plan Orange*, 83.

The Colored War Plans

The JPC carried out planning assignments as directed by the Joint Board, which initially worked on a series of war plans that each focused on the threat presented by one potential enemy. A different color represented each potential enemy. Orange represented Japan, and since planners updated the plans regularly through staff work and exercises, War Plan Orange (WPO) actually consisted of a series of war plans, updated annually through staff work and various practical methods like map exercises. WPO maintained a consistent objective: anticipate any potential Japanese threat and preempt or prevent an attack through offensive operations – essentially defending America by stopping the Japanese military before it could pose a direct threat to the American mainland.[35] In order to fight an offensive war against Japan the United States Navy needed to establish a base in the Far East in order to berth the entire U.S. Fleet. Since only Manila possessed this capability west of Pearl Harbor, war plans directed the Army to defend Manila until the U.S. Fleet arrived to reinforce the Army personnel based there.[36]

American planning during the 1920s and 1930s largely reflected the country's desire to maintain its isolationist policies and avoid entering other nations' wars, leading the United States to enter into a series of treaties during the interwar period. In 1922, the United States signed the first of these treaties: the Five Power Naval Treaty, which called for the United States, Japan, Great Britain, France, and Italy to leave all of their Far Eastern possessions unfortified. In theory, this prevented Japan from fortifying its colony in the Mandate Islands, but more importantly, it ensured Japan did not fortify the Philippines, Guam, and Hong Kong, effectively making the Pacific a free trade zone for naval commerce – including American vessels. Furthermore, the Five

---

[35]Steven T. Ross, *U.S. War Plans 1938-1945* (Boulder: Lynne Rienner Publishers, Inc., 2002), 2.

[36]Munroe McFarlane, "Analysis and Discussion," *Map Problem No. 30, Part 3-Problems and Exercises*, Vol. 55, CAWC 1914-15, Box 5, AWCIR.

Power Treaty included maximum tonnage for each signatory in battleships and battle cruisers: 500,000 for the United States and Great Britain, 300,000 for Japan, and 175,000 each for France and Italy.[37] The major powers intended the Five Powers Treaty and others like it to eliminate the most likely causes of a Pacific war.[38] On the surface, The Five Power Treaty seemed to favor the United States and Great Britain because it allowed them to possess larger fleets of warships. In reality, both the United States and Britain already had larger fleets than the terms of the treaty allowed, and they had to reduce the size of their navies to meet its terms. The United States had to scrap fifteen battleships and battle cruisers. By contrast, the treaty actually left Japan room to grow, and over the coming years, the island nation built up its navy to the maximum allowable tonnage.[39]

In the 1920s, the Board began to develop plans against possible coalitions, including one to defend simultaneously against an attack by Britain and Japan. This plan, known as Plan Red-Orange, led American war planners to consider the challenge posed by formulating a strategy for a two-ocean war – a particularly challenging premise considering it assumed that the United States would wage war without the support of any allies. In accordance with the two-ocean strategy that the war planners developed, the United States would first eliminate the threat in the Atlantic and then turn its attention to the Pacific. According to historian Steven T. Ross, "even though many of the color plans were based upon improbable political scenarios the primary value was that they trained staff officers on the complexity of a major war."[40]

---

[37]Keegan, *Intelligence in War*, 188-89.

[38]Ball, *Of Responsible Command*, 189; Allan R. Millet & Peter Maslowski, *For the Common Defense A Military History of the United States*, 383-84.

[39]Millet and Maslowski, *For the Common Defense*, 383.

[40]Ross, *U.S. War Plans 1938-1945*, 2.

WPO and all of the other color war plans went through many revisions and refinements. The results of war-gaming conducted annually at the Army and Navy War Colleges drove revisions of the WPO by the Joint Army and Navy Board.[41] The War College curricula integrated analysis and testing of all versions of the colored war plans by student committees that provided their recommendations for updating the plans to the Joint Board. These student committees, consisting of senior officers attending their service's War College in preparation for service as colonels (army) or captains (navy), and eventually as flag officers (general or admiral) applied their years of experience to these reviews of the war plans, and their committees did excellent work. For example, Army War College committees identified a number of problems with WPO, including the absence of a defensible system of American bases in the Pacific. Despite the fact that the American fleet possessed technical and numerical superiority over the Imperial Japanese Fleet, it could not operate far beyond its West Coast bases. At that time, the American fleet required large quantities of spare parts, fresh water, food, oil, ammunition, and nearby repair facilities. The Navy responded to these demands by creating "fleet trains" of auxiliary vessels capable of providing mobile support.[42]

Throughout the interwar period the War Department staff and the AWC faculty attempted to add realism to their planning efforts.[43] As the Commandant of the AWC in the early 1930s,

[41]Ball, *Of Responsible Command*, 202.

[42]Millet and Maslowski, *For the Common Defense A Military History of the United States* (New York: The Free Press, 1984), 394.

[43]Ball, *Of Responsible Command*, 235. In 1935, upon General Craig's appointement as Army Chief of Staff, he found that the mobilization plans lacked realism. Ball credited Craig for making a valid assessment, pointing out that America's interwar isolationism had led to under-funding of mobilization bases causing them to erode to such a condition that Post-WWI mobilization plans lacked feasibility. Ball argued that the dynamic international situation required a new national strategy and supporting plans, and demonstrated the Army War College's role in supporting this planning effort.

future Army Chief of Staff General Malin Craig introduced to the curriculum "Current Events" and "Foreign News" under the G2 Division of the college.[44] To add additional realism to the curriculum as events in Europe began to spiral out of control, the AWC in 1940 integrated four Foreign Service Officers into the G2 course.[45] Nevertheless, the G2 course proved to be very unpopular because, as historian Ball has written, "many though it a bother and felt that they were perfectly capable of analyzing international events without their classmates' assistance." Because of consistently negative student feedback, the AWC faculty steadily reduced the length of the G2 course until it only lasted one month. The faculty used the time gained to increase the length of courses that dealt with the command and control of large formations in combat.[46]

Although it shortened the G2 Course, the AWC designed it to add realism to planning committee work by, organizing classes into five working groups, each of which closely following developments in an assigned nation. The faculty also directed students to develop estimates regarding how the policies of these nations affected the United States.[47] Most importantly, however, each of these working groups reviewed war plans from all perspectives – not just that of the nation assigned to them in the G2 Course. All of these changes stemmed from a sweeping AWC curriculum reorganization that took effect in the 1930s, organizing the courses along staff section lines to mimic an actual general staff as closely as possible.[48]

The committee work at the war colleges did suffer from an overly strategic focus, with

---

[44]Henry G. Gole, "War Planning at the War College in the Mid-1930s." *Parameters, Journal of the U.S. Army War College* (January 1984): 55; Ball, *Of Responsible Command*, 239.

[45]Ball, *Of Responsible Command*, 239-40.

[46]Ibid., 202, 239.

[47]Gole, "War Planning at the War College in the Mid-1930s," 55.

[48]Ball, *Of Responsible Command*, 178-201, 247, 250.

plans largely based on strategic intelligence – for example what a nation might do and why (as opposed to how). This led to a neglect of operational art. In the case of WPO, its annual review by the AWC and updating by the War Plan Division staff routinely overlooked at any relevant tactical or operational level factors that would drive the focus of collection for the intelligence organizations in Hawaii. This downward-looking element of the planning function could have significantly benefited the Hawaiian Department's intelligence organizations, particularly regarding their actual capability to detect and provide early warning of a Japanese attack. Instead, detailed planning remained at the discretion of the disparate Hawaiian Departments organizations that did not always have the ability or desire to integrate their efforts. This led to inaccurate estimates of America's own capabilities, blinding war planners to the fact that the Pacific Fleet and the Oahu Garrison lacked the necessary resources to carry out WPO.[49]

In 1939, German aggression in Europe, and Germany's apparent intentions to continue this aggression, led American war planners to shift the U.S. strategic focus from Japan and the Pacific Ocean to Europe and the Atlantic Ocean. War planning moved away from offensive operations toward a concept of defensive operations and readiness, focused – for the time – on the American homeland and its overseas allies. This shift included adoption of a new planning system, the Rainbow Plans, which replaced the colored war plans. Unlike the earlier plans, each of which contemplated war with one nation, or defense of America against a coalition of two or

---

[49]Mark Skinner Watson, *The War Department Chief of Staff: Prewar Plans and Preparations* (Washington D.C.: U.S. Government Printing Office, 1991), 82.; Gudmens, *Staff Ride Handbook*, 42. Senate Joint Committee, *Report on the Investigation of the Pearl Harbor Attack*, Part 15, Joint Committee Exhibits No. 44 through 87; Senate Joint Committee, *Report on the Investigation of the Pearl Harbor Attack*, Part 16, Joint Committee Exhibits No. 88 through 110. In response to the Rainbow Plans, the U.S. Pacific Fleet reorganized itself (See figure 2). In order to execute Rainbow No. 5, Kimmel issued his own plan for its implementation. The Joint Committee investigation record disclosed that from the time the Pacific Fleet arrived at Pearl Harbor until the attack on December 7, both the Army and the Navy high command in Hawaii frequently advised the military authorities in Washington of the shortages in the defense equipment required to safeguard Pearl Harbor.

more enemies, the five new Rainbow Plans contemplated various scenarios in which America would find itself at war against more than one foe and – significantly – in more than one theater of war. This led to a new naming system as well, with the new plans code named Rainbow Plan No. 1, 2, 3, 4, and 5.[50]

Rainbow War Plans

By 1937, the creation of the Axis Alliance (Japan, Germany, and Italy) and other events such as the German occupation of Czechoslovakia and the signing of the Molotov-Ribbentrop Pact caused American war planners to relook their assumptions. In particular, they realized that America could no longer count on only having to fight either a purely defensive war, or a war against only one enemy at a time.[51] In February 1938, the Joint Army and Navy Board approved the last revised WPO.[52] In 1939, operating under the new assumption that the United States would probably have to fight simultaneous campaigns in both the Atlantic and the Pacific, the Joint Board and JPC developed guidelines for the new "Rainbow" plans.[53] The Joint Board directed planners to write the five plans sequentially rather than simultaneously. Further, they directed planners to ensure that each of the five Rainbow plans accounted for an aggressive defense of the Western Hemisphere, along with any offensive or expeditionary elements the plans might include. The shift to the Rainbow Plans marked the end of the United States' passive continental defense strategy.[54]

Rainbow Plan No. 1 rested on the assumption that the United States would fight without

---

[50]Watson, *The War Department Chief of Staff: Prewar Plans and Preparations*, 87, 103.

[51]Gole, *The Road to Rainbow*, 118; Ross, *U.S. War Plans 1938-1945*, 2.

[52]Ball, *Of Responsible Command*, 240.

[53]Hopkins, *The Pacific War*, 27; Miller, *War Plan Orange*, 225.

[54]Ball, *Of Responsible Command*, 241.

any allies, and focused on the defense of the Western Hemisphere south to northern Brazil and west into the Pacific Ocean beyond Hawaii, Wake Island, and American Samoa.[55] In essence, the planners called for the reinforcement of U.S. overseas garrisons, preparation of coastal defense, and concentration of the fleet for action in the Atlantic. Naval squadrons and army reinforcements within reasonably short range of the Hawaiian Department would underwrite the safety and defense of Oahu as a secondary effort.[56] According to historian Steven T. Ross, 'given the size of the United States Navy in 1939 fulfillment of the assigned missions might have been very difficult without extensive mobilization."[57] Moreover, the naval supporting plan for Rainbow Plan No. 1 called for the deployment of most of the fleet to the Caribbean and Brazil, leaving only a few depleted squadrons to guard the Pacific. Another factor that affected the defense planning for Oahu was that the Army did not write a plan to support Rainbow No. 1; instead, it turned to Rainbow No. 4, which focused on preventing the violation of the Monroe Doctrine – e.g. defending all of the territory in the Western Hemisphere.[58]

In Rainbow Plan No. 2, planners focused on the Pacific and assumed that the United States would fight a war with Britain and France as allies. Planners mandated the protection of U.S. vital interests in the region by securing control in the Western Pacific as rapidly as possible.[59] In Rainbow Plan No. 3, planners focused on the Pacific because they assumed that the United States would fight without the assistance of any allies. In essence, Rainbow Plan No. 3 was a version of WPO with the provision that America would prioritize defense of the Western

---

[55]Miller, *War Plan Orange*, 227; Ross, *U.S. War Plans 1938-1945*, 17.

[56]Ross, *U.S. War Plans 1938-1945*, 227.

[57]Ibid., 17.

[58]Miller, *War Plan Orange*, 231; Ross, *U.S. War Plans 1938-1945*, 33, 47.

[59]Miller, *War Plan Orange*, 256; Oral Report of War Plans Group 4, MHI, 5-1935-20.

Hemisphere over any other region. The Joint Board first explored this plan on 3 April 1940, but events in Europe soon forced the Joint Board to wash its hands of Rainbow Plan No. 3 once they acknowledged that the Allies could spare very little combat power for the Pacific until after achieving some success in Europe.[60]

Similar to Rainbow Plan No. 1, planners based Rainbow Plan No. 4 on the same assumption that the United States would fight without allies, but extended the mission to include the defense of the entire Western Hemisphere, east to Greenland and west to the Gilbert Islands. Planners specified the Joint Mission as ensuring the security of the Continental United States, Alaska, Oahu, Panama, the Caribbean Area, and northeastern Brazil to prevent the violation of the letter or spirit of the Monroe Doctrine in all the territory of the Western Hemisphere. Joint Task No.11 of Rainbow Plan No. 4 directed the Army to hold Oahu against attacks by land, sea, and air forces, and against hostile sympathizers, while providing any necessary support the Navy. Additionally, Rainbow Plan No. 4 included both a massive mobilization of the National Guard and Reserves and the introduction of conscription. The plan rested on the assumption "that if and when the French and British fleets fell into Axis hands, the United States would have about six months to prepare for war."[61]

Planners initially anticipated only preparing four Rainbow Plans; however, increasing concerns over Britain's ability to hold out against the Germans forced the Joint Board to elevate Rainbow Plan No. 4 to the status of an emergency defense plan.[62] Planners essentially developed with Rainbow Plan No. 4 an improved hemisphere defense plan. They established a U.S. defensive perimeter that would extend to Cape Horn and to the Atlantic possessions. Fulfilling

---

[60]Miller, *War Plan Orange*, 261, Gole, *The Road to Rainbow*, 118-19;

[61]Ross, *U.S. War Plans 1938-1945*, 33, 47.

[62]Miller, *War Plan Orange*, 214, 231.

just this one task would require two thousand planes continuously patrolling the Western Hemisphere and all of the U.S. outlying possessions. Given that the Navy only had two hundred planes in its inventory at the time, this plan obviously lacked feasibility. Moreover, the dispersion of the Navy fleet specified under Rainbow No. 4 would grant Japan unacceptable freedom of action.[63]

Finally, Rainbow Plan No. 5 planners assumed that the United States would ally with Britain and France and provided for offensive operations by American forces in Europe, Africa, or both.[64] Ultimately U.S. strategic decision makers selected a hybrid of the Rainbow plans known as Plan Dog. The Plan Dog memorandum centered on the primary assessment that the United States should adhere to a Europe First strategy in World War II because of the drastic consequences should Great Britain fall victim to German aggression.[65] This resulted in the Joint Board staff adopting a version of Rainbow Plan No. 5 that involved a two-front war, fighting in both the Atlantic and Pacific Oceans. This plan changed yet again once America entered the war; less than a month before the Pearl Harbor attack the War Department adopted and gained approval for a version of Rainbow Plan No. 5 that codified the "Germany first" policy, which involved U.S. forces dealing with Japan as a secondary threat until the defeat of Germany. It also contained detailed force allocation projections, as well as provisions for combined use of bases in Canada and the United States.[66]

Even though Rainbow Plan No. 5 served as the fundamental underpinning for U.S. policy

---

[63]Ibid., 231.

[64]Ronald H. Spector, *Eagle Against the Sun: The American War with Japan* (New York: The Free Press, 1984), 59.

[65]Gole, *The Road to Rainbow*, 114; Miller, *War Plan Orange,* 270; Millet and Maslowski, *For the Common Defense*, 418; Ross, *U.S. War Plans 1938-1945*, 55.

[66]Ross, *U.S. War Plans 1938-1945*, 135.

guiding World War II strategy, President Roosevelt only gave oral approval for the plan.[67] Rainbow No. 5 called for the defeat of Germany, beginning with a holding action in the Pacific before implementing WPO.[68] Given Germany's status as the main enemy, the Pacific would remain a secondary theater until its defeat.[69] Therefore, the U.S. mission in the Pacific took on a strategically defensive posture focused on protecting shipping on the Pacific.[70] Because of the Germany-first policy, the defense of Hawaii received low priority for resources. Planners envisioned a two-year limited war in the Pacific, at which point they envisioned the defeat of Germany and a shift of focus to Japan. They hoped that this limited war would cost America relatively little by exploiting Japan's economic vulnerabilities.[71]

Under the Rainbow plan system, American planners addressed a wide range of potential war scenarios. The planners based the development of Rainbow Plans No. 1 through No. 4 on the central assumption that the Untied States would explicitly dedicate all its energy and resources primarily to the European Theater of Operations. Because of this focus, planning for the Pacific continued to lack operational and tactical detail, and the Hawaiian Department did not receive the resources it required to implement war plans in the Pacific. These issues ultimately hindered planning for the Hawaiian department in terms of the appropriateness of the planning to the actual situation on hand in Hawaii and its garrison's ability to execute the plan.

---

[67]Millet and Maslowski, *For the Common Defense*, 2.

[68]Hopkins, *The Pacific War*, 2.

[69]Ibid., 33.

[70]Miller, *War Plan Orange,* 314

[71]Ibid., 315.

Rainbow War Plans			
Rainbow Plan	**Allies**	**Primary Area**	**Secondary Area**
1	None	Atlantic	Pacific
2	Britain, France	Pacific	Atlantic (Limited)
3	None	Pacific	Atlantic
4	None	South Atlantic	Pacific
5	Britain, France	Atlantic	Pacific

Figure 1. Rainbow War Plans.

Source: Jeffrey J. Gudmens, *Staff Ride Handbook for the Attack on Pearl Harbor, 7 December 1941: A Study of Defending America* (Fort Leavenworth: Combat Studies Institute Press, 1960), 40.

OAHU DEFENSE PLAN

Given the evolution of strategic plans and the Pacific's sudden re-designation as a low-priority effort, Kimmel reorganized the Pacific Fleet for maximum efficiency (See figure 2), and Hawaiian department planners from Army and Navy units developed an Oahu defense plan known as the "Joint Coastal Frontier Defense Plan," largely based on concepts included in Rainbow Plan No. 1.[72] Admiral Isoroku Yamamoto, the principal planner for the attack on Pearl Harbor and commander in chief of the Japanese Combined Fleet faced a formidable foe when he decided to target the island of Oahu. Nevertheless, the United States overestimated its own capabilities in defending the island; Roosevelt and American military leaders considered Oahu an impregnable fortification.[73] The Army Chief of Staff General Marshall expressed to President Roosevelt in May 1941:

---

[72]Gudmens, *Staff Ride Handbook*, 42; Miller, *War Plan Orange,* 314; Wohlstetter, *Pearl Harbor,* 340.

[73]Wohlstetter, *Pearl Harbor*, 69; Senate Joint Committee, *Report on the Investigation of the Pearl Harbor Attack*, Part 15, 546; Freeman, *Pearl Harbor*, 244; Kent G. Budge. "Pearl Harbor, The Pacific War Online Encyclopedia, 2007." http://pwencycl.kgbudge.com/P/e/Pearl_ Harbor.htm (accessed 28 January 2013).

The island of Oahu [the island on which Pearl Harbor is located], due to its fortification, its garrison and its physical characteristics, is believed to be the strongest fortress in the world. In addition, Hawaii is capable of reinforcement by heavy bombers from the mainland by air. With this force available, a major attack against Oahu is considered impracticable.[74]

In reality, Japan faced an island that was not prepared or able to defend itself against an attack. American decision makers overestimated the Hawaiian Department's capabilities, assessing that the U.S. had ten times more capability than Japan to wage war.[75] As a result, the Hawaiian Department did not receive adequate numbers of personnel or equipment to develop a powerful, well-coordinated, and integrated defense system in accordance with their longstanding plans, based on the interwar assumption that the main effort would consist of the U.S. war against Japan.

The Hawaiian island of Oahu held a position of importance for the United States long before World War II. During the interwar years, Oahu and the Panama Canal Zone served as key parts of the American continental defense system. [76] As long as the United States Navy kept the bulk of its fleet in the eastern Pacific, neither Japan nor any other nation had the strength to establishing a hostile base from which to launch major operations against the hemisphere's Pacific front.[77] Rainbow Plan No. 5 included Pearl Harbor within the area defined as the Hawaiian Coastal Frontier. The plan further divided responsibility for the defense of the Hawaiian Coastal Frontier between the Commanding General of the Hawaiian Department (Army), and the

---

[74]Freeman, *Pearl Harbor*, 244; Wohlstetter, *Pearl Harbor*, 69; Senate Joint Committee, *Report on the Investigation of the Pearl Harbor Attack*, Part 15.

[75]Wohlstetter, *Pearl Harbor*, 355.

[76]Miller, *War Plan Orange*, 10; Ball, *Of Responsible Command*, 190; Stetson Conn, Rose C. Engelman, and Byron Fairchild, *Guarding The United States and Its Outposts* (Washington D.C.: U.S. Government Printing Office, 2000), 150; Watson, *Chief of Staff: Prewar Plans and Preparations*, 465-66.

[77]Wohlstetter, *Pearl Harbor*, 26; Conn, Engelman, and Fairchild, *Guarding The United States and its Outposts*, 150.

Commandant of the 14th Naval District (Navy). The Navy commander, designated the Commander of the Hawaiian Naval Coastal Frontier, led the naval local defense force, and coordinated its joint tactical and strategic employment with the Hawaiian Department.[78]

The War Department in 1920 defined the mission of the Hawaiian Department's army forces as the defense of the Pearl Harbor naval base against "damage from naval or aerial bombardment or by enemy sympathizers" and against "attack by enemy expeditionary force or forces, supported or unsupported by an enemy fleet or fleets."[79] The Army thus had primary responsibility for the protection of Pearl Harbor. To fulfill this responsibility before World War II the Army maintained on Oahu its largest, and in some respects, its best-equipped overseas garrison.[80] The mission remained essentially unchanged until February 1941, when General Marshall informally broadened the Army's stated mission by emphasizing the responsibility of the Army for protecting the Pacific Fleet as well as the Pearl Harbor naval installations.[81]

As the situation in Europe worsened, planning for the defense in Oahu continued. On 11 April 1941, General Short and Admiral Block (acting on behalf of Kimmel) published the most comprehensive defense plan to date for Hawaii, the Joint Coastal Frontier Defense Plan (JCFDP). This "gentlemen's agreement" delineated the areas of responsibility and tasks, established a Joint

---

[78]Senate Joint Committee, *Report of the Joint Committee on the Investigation of the Pearl Harbor Attack*, Part 15, Joint Committee Exhibits No. 44 through 87.

[79]Conn, Engelman, and Fairchild, *Guarding The United States and its Outposts*, 150; Wohlstetter, *Pearl Harbor*, 19; Ross, *U.S. War Plans 1938 – 1945*, 47.

[80]Watson, *Chief of Staff: Prewar Plans and Preparations*, 465-66; Conn, Engelman, and Fairchild, *Guarding The United States and its Outposts*, 150-51, 470; "Statement of Rear Admiral Husband E. Kimmel, Before the Joint Committee on the Investigation of the Pearl Harbor Attack, 15-21 November 1945." http://www.pearlharbor911attacks.com/old/docs/ HEK_JCC_STATEMENT_11546.pdf (accessed 27 January 2013).

[81]Conn, Engelman, and Fairchild, *Guarding The United States and its Outposts*, 150-51; Miller, *War Plan Orange*, 314.

Planning Committee to continue joint planning, and required each service to write supporting defensive plans.[82] Because of the JCFDP both services had fairly adequate joint plans that clearly delineated responsibilities, and sought to compensate for the shortages and weakness of the other services while capitalizing on their strengths.

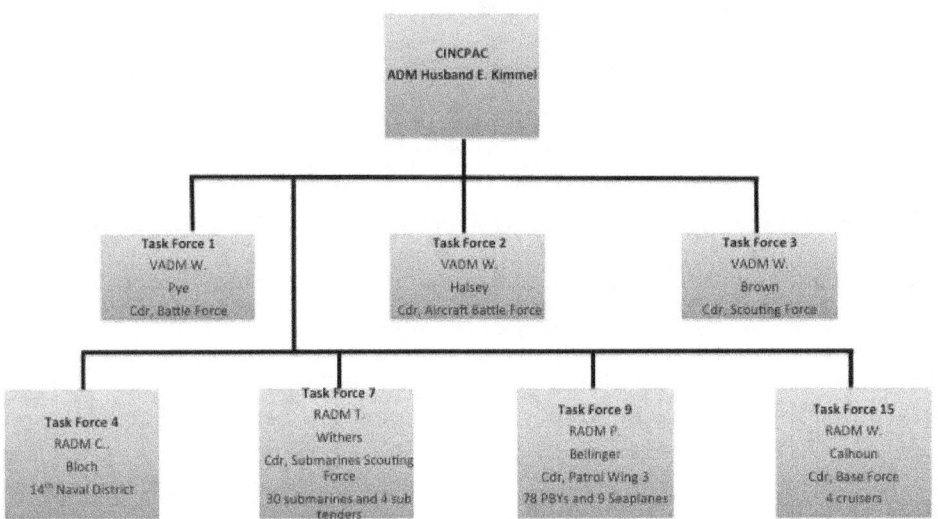

Figure 2. Pacific Fleet Organization December 7, 1941.

Source: Jeffrey J. Gudmens, Staff Ride Handbook for the Attack on Pearl Harbor, 7 December 1941: A Study of Defending America, (Fort Leavenworth: Combat Studies Institute Press, 1960), 42.

However, the plans had two major flaws: they depended on early warning and detection, and timely and accurate intelligence.[83] Lack of adequate equipment created a challenge for early warning and detection. Making matters worse, forces lacked the ability to conduct reliable target discrimination between friendly and foe, and each service had its own alert system that it would execute once consensus finally existed that surveillance forces had detected a threat.[84]

---

[82]Wohlstetter, *Pearl Harbor*, 19;. Gudmens, *Staff Ride Handbook*, 90.

[83]Gudmens, *Staff Ride Handbook*, 90.

[84]Ibid., 94. The Army and Navy each had an established system of alerts with severity

The plan entitled the "Joint Action of the Army and Navy, 1935" described the roles and relationships of the Army and Navy in the formulation of defense plans for the Hawaiian Islands.[85] The allocation of Army and Navy responsibility for coastal defense under the conditions in Hawaii made that mission unachievable. Fundamental deficiencies in equipment, particularly the lack of sufficient Army patrol planes and available radar equipment, created significant limitations.[86] The Army and Navy recognized and attempted to compensate for such shortfalls in early 1941 with a series of defense plans known as the Joint Coastal Frontier Defense Plan and the Hawaiian Coastal Defense. Short and Block, signed and placed in effect the plan on April 11, 1941. This plan was the based on the joint Army and Navy basic war plan Orange and operations plan Rainbow Plan No 5 as described above.[87]

The defense of Oahu centered on four key capabilities. These included the natural defensive strength of Pearl Harbor, anti-aircraft equipment, torpedo nets and baffles, and lastly radar equipment.[88] Planners believed that these four capabilities would ensure not only protection of the island from enemy aerial and naval attacks, but early warning of an attack to allow sufficient time for friendly forces to respond. However, an enemy could approach Pearl Harbor from all directions; in order to counter this, the Army established a mutually supporting system of

levels of one through three. In the Army's system, level one represented the least significant threat, while for the Navy it represented the most significant. Neither service knew this difference existed in their emergency alert systems.

[85]Senate Joint Committee, *Report on the Investigation of the Pearl Harbor Attack*, Part 15, 82-83.

[86]Ibid.

[87]Senate Committee, *Hearings Before the Joint Committee on the Investigation of the Pearl Harbor Attack*, 39 vols. 79th Cong., 1st sess., 1946, Part I, November 15-17 and 19-21; "Statement of Rear Admiral Kimmel," http://www.pearlharbor911attacks.com/old/docs/ HEK_JCC_STATEMENT_11546.pdf (accessed 27 January 2013).

[88]*Report of the Joint Committee on the Investigation of the Pearl Harbor Attack, Executive Summary*, 544-46.

coastal defense.[89] For more than a century before the attack, the Army employed harbor defense as its primary means to defend its seacoast. The harbor defense consisted of bases equipped with permanently installed guns of various calibers. In case of an attack or other type of emergency, mobile coastal artillery and minefields would augment the guns. The harbor defense served the purpose of guarding the area against invasion and capture, protecting against naval bombardment, submarine or surface torpedo attack, and covering the seaward approaches to a great enough distance from Oahu to permit Untied States Navy ships to respond.[90] However, coastal defense systems such as this one never lived up to the promises of Coast Artillery personnel.

The Army's air bases at Wheeler Field, Hickam Field, and Bellows Field provided the principle means of the Oahu defense plan, written by the Hawaiian Department G3 and synchronized with the ever-changing colored plans focused on the defense of America from attack by other world powers.[91] In late May 1940, President Roosevelt ordered the Pacific Fleet to remain in Pearl Harbor after the completion of Fleet Problem XXI. (The Pacific Fleet was previously was based in San Diego, California, with Pearl Harbor serving as an advanced deployment base.) Roosevelt hoped it would act as some sort of deterrent against an attack.[92] Hawaiian Department personnel expected long distance patrol planes to provide reconnaissance

---

[89]Ibid., 82-83.

[90]Conn, Engelman, and Fairchild, *Guarding the Untied States and Its Outposts*, 45.

[91]Mark T. Calhoun, "Lesley J. McNair: Little-Known Architect of the U.S. Army" (lecture, University of Kansas Hall Center, Lawrence, March 4, 2011); Wohlstetter, *Pearl Harbor*, 410; Conn, Engelman, and Fairchild, *Guarding The United States and its Outposts*, 150; *Report of the Joint Committee on the Investigation of the Pearl Harbor Attack, Executive Summary*, 62.

[92]Miller, *War Plan Orange*, 219; *Report of the Joint Committee on the Investigation of the Pearl Harbor Attack, Executive Summary*, 545; Robert J. Hanyok, "How the Japanese Did It." *Naval History Magazine* 23, no. 6, December 2009, http://www.usni.org/magazines/navalhistory /2009-12/how-japanese-did-it. (accessed 28 January 2013); Prange, *At Dawn We Slept*, 37-39.

coverage in a 360-degree perimeter around Oahu.[93] The base defense required approximately 175

planes, However, only 13 were present at the time of the attack, only 6 of these were

operational.[94] This is but one example of the disparity between the planning concept and the

Hawaiian Department's operational capability in reality.

Due to its diminutive size and complex terrain, Pearl Harbor could not station all the

forces necessary for its own defense, much less the defense of Oahu.[95] This required dispersal of

assets, which improved their survivability during an attack and improved the speed with which

they could get airborne since each runway supported fewer aircraft. However, this dispersal

complicated command and control of these forces because under the JCFDP many units that

reported to a variety of commands bore the responsibility for the defense of Oahu, and these

forces had difficulty maintaining communications over the space that separated them.[96]

Moreover, delays occurred in relative respond times after notification because aircraft located at

Wheeler Field, Hickam Field, and Bellows Field had to fly varying distances and receive

instructions from different communications stations before arriving where needed to join the

defense. Further, a breakdown existed between theory and reality. Pilots could count on only

thirty minutes' notification of an attack, but required one to two hours to scramble and launch.

This reality did not bode well for a military response in the event of an attack.

Antiaircraft batteries with appropriate and sufficient ammunition and experienced crew to

---

[93]Wohlstetter, *Pearl Harbor*, 13; Congress of the United States Executive Summary Investigation of the Pearl Harbor Attack, 62.

[94]Senate Joint Committee, *Report of the Joint Committee on the Investigation of the Pearl Harbor Attack, Executive Summary*, 62; Watson, *Chief of Staff: Prewar Plans and Preparations*, 474; Wohlstetter, *Pearl Harbor*, 26.

[95]Conn, Engelman, and Fairchild, *Guarding The United States and its Outposts*, 153-54.

[96] Prange, *At Dawn We Slept*, 404; Stinnett, *Day of Deceit*, 238-39; Clausen and Lee, *Pearl Harbor*, 72; Wohlstetter, *Pearl Harbor*, 8.

operate them formed the second layer of defense.[97] Questions remain regarding the adequacy of the antiaircraft batteries and supplies available at Pearl Harbor on December 7. Regardless, with almost none of batteries on alert at any given time, this layer of defense faced similar challenges as defending aircraft. Making matters worse, these batteries lacked adequate and readily available ammunition to enable an effective response to an attack.[98]

Torpedo nets and baffles provided adequate protection for the Pacific Fleet at all times – particularly during fueling and repair activities.[99] The success an attack on Pearl Harbor depended on the attacking forces' ability to utilize torpedoes launched by aircraft in shallow waters and to drop bombs accurately on "point target as opposed to area targets."[100] At the time, Japanese aviators could only achieve a torpedo attack by conducting low-level torpedo drops because of the lack of modern aiming devices, and limited load capacities of their planes. Planners believed torpedo nets, baffles, and barrage balloons provided adequate protection against this type of attack.[101] Based on this assessment of the contemporary state of torpedo attack and defense capability, both Kimmel and Bloch – referring to their staffs' assessments, argued that the "danger of a successful torpedo attack on Pearl Harbor was negligible."[102] Bafflingly, even after

---

[97]Senate Joint Committee, *Report of the Joint Committee on the Investigation of the Pearl Harbor Attack, Executive Summary*, 544-46.

[98]Fairchild, *Guarding The United States and Its Outposts*, 60; Senate Joint Committee, *Report of the Joint Committee on the Investigation of the Pearl Harbor Attack*, Executive Summary, 548.

[99]Senate Joint Committee, *Report of the Joint Committee on the Investigation of the Pearl Harbor Attack*, Executive Summary, 544-46.

[100]Eliot A. Cohen and John Gooch, *Military Misfortunes The Anatomy of Failure in War* (New York: Vintage Books, 1990), 50.

[101]Ibid. Barrage balloons consisted of air-filled bags attached to steel cables, intended to create obstacles that would deny low-level airspace to enemy aircraft.

[102]Wohlstetter, *Pearl Harbor*, 370.

identifying their importance through this assessment, U.S. forces on Oahu chose not to emplace

anti-torpedo nets because they would limit the maneuver room for ships. In addition to the

congestion that they would cause, the expense and difficulty of installing the nets presented an

additional rationale for not employing them.[103]

Most defense planners deemed the final layer of defense, the recently fielded radar,

sufficiently perfected to provide early warning of approaching planes as far as 100 miles or more

away from the island.[104] The JCFP required the Army to establish the Aircraft Warning System

(AWS), which should, in theory, provide early warning and detection of incoming enemy.[105] As

early as December 1939, the Army established an Aircraft Warning Service (AWS) that relied on

radar for the defense of American territories, including Hawaii.[106] The U.S. government had

reason to trust in the capability of radar. Starting in 1935, Britain installed a series of radar

stations on the southern coast of England.[107] These stations proved to be a major factor in

winning the Battle of Britain. Beginning in 1940, England and the United States collaborated to

further develop and refine radar systems.[108] This collaboration enabled U.S. political and military

---

[103]Senate Committee, *Hearings Before the Joint Committee on the Investigation of the Pearl Harbor Attack*, 545, 1318; Wohlstetter, *Pearl Harbor: Warning and Decision,* 370. On November 22, 1922 Admiral Stark wrote a memorandum to Admiral Richardson in which he expressed his concern about the lack of torpedo net protection. Richardson did not share Starks's concerns and believed torpedo nets did not serve any useful purpose.

[104]"Statement of Rear Admiral Kimmel," http://www.pearlharbor911attacks.com/old/ docs/HEK_JCC_STATEMENT_11546.pdf (accessed 27 January 2013); Senate Joint Committee, *Report of the Joint Committee on the Investigation of the Pearl Harbor Attack*, 544-46.

[105]Gudmens, *Staff Ride Handbook*, 90.

[106]Wohlstetter, *Pearl Harbor*, 6-12; Harry A. Butowsky. "Early Warnings: The Mystery of Radar in Hawaii." Cultural Resource Management 23, no. 3 (January 1999): 4.

[107]Harry A. Butowsky. "Early Warnings: The Mystery of Radar in Hawaii." *Cultural Resource Management* 23, no. 3 (January 1999): 4.

[108]Clausen and Lee, *Pearl Harbor*, 92; Butowsky, "Early Warnings": 4.

leaders to see the potential in radar, and led the Secretary of War to approve establishment of the AWS.

The Army established direction mobile radar detector (SCR-270) sets at six locations on Oahu: Kawaiola, Waianae, Kaawa, Koko Head, Schofield Barracks, and Fort Shafter.[109] The AWS relied on a centralized information center at Fort Shafter. Personnel at this center plotted the location of incoming planes based on the information provided from the six radar stations located on the island, in theory providing early warning of approaching aircraft.[110] Two key problems limited the effectiveness of the information center at Fort Shafter, however. Personnel there only plotted the recorded positions of planes picked up by the radarscope – not the projected positions over time – and they had no way to distinguish between friendly and enemy planes.[111]

The planners at the Hawaiian Department intended the radar sets on Oahu to make up only one component of an integrated air defense system. They intended for the six mobile long-range radar installations of the AWS, the Aircraft Warning Communications net, and the Aircraft Information center to operate as one integrated unit.[112] The radar system seemed promising after testing of the radars in Waianae and Koko Head, which proved able to detect planes at a range of eighty-five miles.[113] The Army and Navy conducted several subsequent drills in November 1941

---

[109]Senate Joint Committee, *Report of the Joint Committee on the Investigation of the Pearl Harbor Attack,* Part 27, 322; Wohlstetter, *Pearl Harbor,* 6; Gudmens, *Staff Ride Handbook,* 91.

[110]Wohlstetter, *Pearl Harbor,* 6;. Prange, *At Dawn We Slept,* 500.

[111]Stinnett, *Day of Deceit,* 237-38; Prange, *At Dawn We Slept,* 500.

[112] Prange, *At Dawn We Slept,* 42; Stinnett, *Day of Deceit,* 239.

[113]Trefousse, *What Happened at Pearl Harbor?*, 131; Butowsky. "Early Warnings": 4; Clausen and Lee, *Pearl Harbor,* 72.

to test the readiness of the response plan, but these drills did not provide conclusive results.[114] For example, none of the drills took place with all of the radar centers manned simultaneously.[115]

Further complicating matters, much transformation took place in the Army Air Corps and the Army Anti-Aircraft Artillery Batteries between 1939 and 1941. The Army Air Corps converted its pursuit squadrons into interceptor squadrons for a planned Interceptor Command. Anti-Aircraft Artillery batteries required modernization to enable the employment of their new SCR-268 radars.[116] By December 1941, the integration of these commands, missions, and modernization remained incomplete. In the words of historians Henry C. Clausen and Bruce Lee, "An integrated air defense command system had not been established."[117] Because of the lack of an integrated air defense system, at this late stage, the defenders of Pearl Harbor still could not synchronize their efforts against an air attack – neither aerial nor radar-based long-range reconnaissance provided the required capability. Furthermore, the lack of integrated defense significantly delayed Oahu's defense forces' response time when attempting to mobilize fighter squadrons and get them airborne, or man antiaircraft guns positions.[118]

As established, the air defense and radar systems in Oahu could not provide sufficient early warning to anticipate and preempt or prevent a surprise attack. As operated, the radar system provided little protection because it failed to provide what it promised: early warning. The radar system suffered from many limitations, including limited hours of operation. The aircraft

---

[114]Prange, *At Dawn We Slept*, 243-44; Stinnett, *Day of Deceit*, 149-50; Wohlstetter, *Pearl Harbor*, 9.

[115]Wohlstetter, *Pearl Harbor*, 9.

[116]Butowsky. "Early Warnings": 4.

[117]Clausen and Lee, *Pearl Harbor*, 204; Wohlstetter, *Pearl Harbor*, 8.

[118]Clausen and Lee, *Pearl Harbor*, 204.

control and warning (ACW) system only operated for four hours daily, and even then only on a training basis.[119] Short instituted the hours of operation based on a war warning issued by the War Department in Washington, rather than real-world intelligence indicators in the Pacific.[120]

The Army's Aircraft Warning Service (AWS) also lacked a reliable mode of communications between the information center and the various operation centers, some of which possessed no means of communicating warnings or sightings to the information center.[121] The ACW continued to operate in a training mode throughout 1941 because it was still learning how to use recently received equipment, and because commanders hesitated to modify the established command and control relationships of the units in training by assigning them to operational headquarters.[122] The ACW received new mobile radars in August 1941, and continued to operate in coordination with a temporary information center.[123] The head of the Signal Corps, Colonel Powell, retained operational control of the unit as long as it remained in training status, and he steadfastly refused to relinquish control.[124]

Because of these various factors, the radars provided inadequate early warning to facilitate an effective defense of Oahu. Historians generally agree that the radar system could detect planes from about 100 to 150 miles away.[125] Based on airspeeds and notification times, this

---

[119]Stinnett, *Day of Deceit*, 238; Wohlstetter, *Pearl Harbor,* 8; Clausen and Lee, *Pearl Harbor*, 73.

[120]Wohlstetter, *Pearl Harbor,* 10; Clausen and Lee, *Pearl Harbor*, 232.

[121]Prange, *At Dawn We Slept*, 404; Stinnett, *Day of Deceit*, 238-39; Clausen and Lee, *Pearl Harbor*, 72; Wohlstetter, *Pearl Harbor,* 8.

[122]Clausen and Lee, *Pearl Harbor*, 73; Wohlstetter, *Pearl Harbor*, 8-9.

[123]Wohlstetter, *Pearl Harbor*, 8.

[124]Ibid., 9.

[125]Stinnett, *Day of Deceit*, 237; Clausen and Lee, *Pearl Harbor*, 92; Wohlstetter, *Pearl*

meant Short received word of approaching planes approximately one hour before their projected arrival. However, this only accounted for notifying aircraft squadrons and getting fighters airborne by the time enemy planes arrived at the island. Notifying fighter squadrons and dispatching them to intercept aircraft before they reached Oahu required about an hour or two. In other words, Short only had about 30 minutes from the time the radar detected the enemy's planes before he had to get his planes into the air in order to avert an attack.[126] This still made interception feasible, if only barely, but the lack of a fully integrated and functioning command center capable of making a timely decision to launch made interdiction all but impossible.[127]

PRE-WAR U.S. INTELLIGENCE COMMUNITY

In the words of one analyst, numerous examples "demonstrate that not all national decision makers and commanders in Pearl Harbor had access to the same information or intelligence regarding the imminent attack."[128] However, one can argue that no decision maker or leader ever possesses perfect or complete intelligence. Regardless, in the absence of perfect intelligence those leaders can mitigate uncertainty – in fact, success often relies on the ability to plan in the absence of intelligence. Leaders do have the ability to evaluate the intelligence or information at hand and derive from that information reasonable conclusions. Most importantly, though, effective leaders share their findings and take effective action based on their conclusions.

The United States intelligence community before America's direct involvement in World War II consisted of several semi-independent organizations. These organizations competed for

---

Harbor, 8.

[126]Cohen and Gooch, *Military Misfortunes*, 48; Gudmens, *Staff Ride Handbook*, 92; Freeman, *Pearl Harbor*, 277.

[127]Clausen and Lee, *Pearl Harbor*, 204; Wohlstetter, *Pearl Harbor*, 8.

[128]Robert F. Piacine, "Pearl Harbor: Failure of Intelligence" (master's thesis, Air War College, 1997), 48.

limited resources and often shared overlapping collection and intelligence evaluation responsibilities and functions.[129] Despite these obstacles, the intelligence produced by these organizations consistently indicated that Japan intended to seize the resource-rich territories in Southeast Asia.[130] These organizations also consistently warned the U.S. government that Japan harbored ever-growing hostile intentions towards the United States, with indicators centering on Pearl Harbor as a potential target.[131] In order to understand and assess American intelligence capabilities that existed before the attack on Pearl Harbor, one must comprehend what U.S. intelligence organizations and capabilities existed there before the attack. Further, one must consider what intelligence sources and methods U.S. organizations utilized in order to assist military decision makers before 7 December 1941.

Intelligence Groups in Hawaii

Before the beginning of the war in the Pacific, five major U.S. intelligence organizations existed: (1) the Office of Naval Intelligence (ONI or OP-16), (2) the Army's Military Intelligence Division (MID or G-2), (3) the Federal Bureau of Investigation (FBI), (4) the State Department, and (5) the Office of the Coordinator of Information (COI). Each of these organizations collected, evaluated and disseminated information to senior leadership within their respective government agency and through the executive branch to President Franklin D. Roosevelt. During this period, other agencies acted as intelligence collectors, such as the Office of Naval Communications (OP-

---

[129]Clausen and Lee, *Pearl Harbor*, 45-46.

[130]Prange, *At Dawn We Slept*, 4.

[131]Fredrick D. Parker, *Pearl Harbor Revisited: United States Navy Communications Intelligence 1924-194 Series IV World War II Volume 6* (Fort Meade: National Security Agency, 1994), 26; Ross, *U.S. War Plans 1938-1945*, 2. Throughout the 1930s Joint Board war planners consistently found an attack against Pearl Harbor far more likely than one against the mainland.

20) and military attachés, but they did not conduct intelligence evaluations.[132]

Each of these intelligence organizations had their own divisions with specific roles to include the collection, evaluation to support their service mission requirements and dissemination of intelligence to their own department chief and in some case to the office of the President of the United States. Together these organizations furnished the majority of the intelligence available to national and military decision makers before the Japanese attack on Pearl Harbor.[133]

Navy Intelligence Organizations

The Navy's primary intelligence organization at Pearl Harbor, the Office of Naval Intelligence (ONI) or OP-16, worked for the Chief of Naval Operations (CNO). The Hawaiian office consisted of three divisions: Combat Intelligence under Lieutenant Commander Joseph J. Rochefort, Fleet Intelligence under Lieutenant Commander Edwin T. Layton, and Counterespionage under Captain Irving Mayfield. Mayfield was the 14th District Intelligence officer and reported directly to Admiral Bloch (the commandant of the 14th Naval District). Rochefort's unit served under the command of the 14th District, while Layton served under Admiral Kimmel's command (Commander in Chief, Pacific Fleet).[134]

The 14th District Combat Intelligence Section worked closely with its partner Far Eastern field unit, the 16th Naval District (each of which maintained its main office in Washington). Each unit received its orders regarding collection and intelligence priorities from Washington. The two Combat Intelligence sections sent any intelligence they collected to the Chief of Naval Operations, the Commander in Chief Asiatic Fleet, and the Commander in Chief U.S. Fleet – but

---

[132]Wohlstetter, *Pearl Harbor*, 28-29.

[133]Senate Joint Committee, *Report of the Joint Committee on the Investigation of the Pearl Harbor Attack*, Part 32, 369.

[134]Ibid., 31.

most importantly, they shared intelligence with each other. The 14th District focused on conducting radio traffic analysis to determine the locations of Japanese ships, while the 16th District sought both to determine the locations of Japanese ships and to intercept and decode Japanese diplomatic traffic (code name Magic).

Army Intelligence Organizations

Two Army intelligence organizations operated in Hawaii: the G2 office of the Hawaiian Department staff headed by Lieutenant Colonel Kendall J. Fielder (and his assistant Lieutenant Colonel George W. Bicknell) and a special G2 unit for the Army Air Corps headed by Colonel Edward W. Raley. Fiedler and Bicknell reported directly to General Short (Commander in Chief Hawaiian Department), while Colonel Raley reported directly to Major General F.L. Martin (Army Air Corps Commander). The G2 contained three sections, an administrative section, a public relations section, and two counter-intelligence sections (one led by Bicknell). The Signal Intelligence Service (SIS), led by Colonel William F. Freidman also collected intelligence, although it did not work for the G2.

According to 1940 Army regulations, the G2 performed "those duties…which relate to the collection, evaluation, and dissemination of military information."[135] Therefore, the G2 offices in Hawaii performed the primary functions of interpreting and exploiting open source intelligence, and conducting counter-intelligence activities. The received much of their intelligence by debriefing businessmen returning from the Orient in order to obtain any information that they might have on the general situation in the Pacific area.[136] The G2 office also conducted interviews of British officials and military representatives of other nations who

---

[135]Senate Committee, *Hearings Before the Joint Committee on the Investigation of the Pearl Harbor Attack*, Part 27, 1419; Wohlstetter, *Pearl Harbor*, 290.

[136]Prange, *At Dawn We Slept*, 79.

traveled through Hawaii, conducting intercepts of all Japanese plain language radio broadcasts, monitored local Japanese-language newspapers, and followed select newspapers from the Orient.[137] They focused primarily on local subversive activities, but limited themselves to estimating capabilities rather than intentions. The Army G2 office was performed the interception and decoding of Japanese diplomatic traffic code. The SIS intercepted, decrypted, and translated foreign diplomatic and military communications, code-named Purple.

DUE TO COPYRIGHT RESTRICTIONS
SOME OR ALL IMAGES ARE NOT INCLUDED

Figure 3. Army and Navy Intelligence Structure and Communication Sharing Channels.

Source: Roberta Wohlstetter, *Pearl Harbor Warning and Decision,* (Stanford: Stanford University Press, 1962), 29.

Federal Bureau of Investigation

At this time, the Federal Bureau of Investigation (FBI) performed the primary mission of counterespionage. The Attorney General's office tasked the FBI with taking charge of

---

[137]Senate Committee, *Hearings Before the Joint Committee on the Investigation of the Pearl Harbor Attack*, Part 10, 5119; Wohlstetter, *Pearl Harbor,* 37.

investigating work in matters relating to espionage, sabotage, and violations of the neutrality regulations.[138] The FBI conducted operations in support of Pearl Harbor from two locations: Honolulu and Washington D.C. During this period, Robert L. Shivers – himself a nineteen-year veteran of the Bureau – headed the FBI in Hawaii.[139] The FBI' Honolulu office focused on surveillance and reporting on the activities of the personnel assigned to the Honolulu Consulate and the Japanese Embassy staff. Honolulu Consulate FBI agents' observation methods included the monitoring of wire tapes on both official and unofficial telephone lines. Agent Shiver's Honolulu office handled all cases of subversive activity (including espionage) involving the general civilian population.[140] In the case of Japanese subjects, the FBI shared concurrent authority and responsibility with the Navy District Intelligence Office (DIO) for the monitoring of the activities of Japanese employees assigned to the Honolulu consulate. Shivers' office also maintained contact and exchanged relevant intelligence with the Army's Hawaiian G2 section, while sharing concurrent authority and responsibility with the Navy District Intelligence Office (DIO). By all accounts, a cordial working relationship existed between the FBI and service intelligence offices. Most importantly, the organizations shared intelligence freely and effectively. Bicknell (Assistant G2 office for the Hawaiian Department) worked out of the Federal Building, which meant a key member of the Hawaiian Department's military staff co-located with Shivers and his small staff. In addition, every Tuesday Shivers, Bicknell, and Mayfield (14th District Intelligence officer) met to exchange information.[141]

---

[138] Ameringer, *U.S. Foreign Intelligence: The Secret Side of American History* (Lexington: Lexington Books, 1990), 133.

[139] Prange, *At Dawn We Slept*, 78.

[140] Wohlstetter, *Pearl Harbor*, 35-36.

[141] Prange, *At Dawn We Slept*, 78, 80.

State Department

The president named Henry L. Stimson Secretary of State in 1929. The Cipher Bureau, otherwise known as the Black Chamber, served as the United States' first peacetime cryptanalytic organization and a forerunner of the National Security Agency.[142] Secretary Stimson called the operations "unethical and stated that gentlemen do not read each others' mail."[143] Stimson soon terminated the State Department's cryptologic activities and formally transferred the MI-8 to the Army.[144] He shut down the Black Chamber upon learning that the State Department lacked the funding to operate it. This meant that American ambassadors and their embassy staffs provided the main source of intelligence collection and reporting for the State Department.

Ambassador Joseph C. Grew served as the head of the United States embassy in Tokyo in the period leading up to the Pearl Harbor attack.[145] Ambassador Grew, a senior career diplomat, spent nine years in Japan, but he never mastered the Japanese language (unlike his wife Alice Grew, granddaughter of Commodore Perry). According to historian Gordon W. Prange, despite this shortcoming Ambassador Grew became "a shrewd observer of the Japanese scene and called the shots as he saw them."[146] The Ambassador focused on reporting political and economic rather than military information. These reports also included the observations from military attaches assigned to the embassy.

---

[142]Parker, *Pearl Harbor Revisited*, 13.

[143]Clausen and Lee, *Pearl Harbor*, 39.

[144]David Kahn, *The Code Breakers: The Comprehensive History of Secret Communications from Ancient Times to the Internet* (New York: Scribner Book Co., 1996), 484. After World War I the War Office established the Cryptanalytic Agency under the Military Intelligence Division.

[145]Stinnett, *Day of Deceit*, 10; Prange, *At Dawn We Slept*, 4.

[146]Prange, *At Dawn We Slept*, 7.

Although the ambassador's and the attaches' reports could not give specific reporting on military and naval movements or provide time-sensitive intelligence that could have averted the attack at Pearl Harbor, by January 24, 1940 Grew's office learned of Japan's initial attack plans.[147] A member of the State Department, Max W. Bishop did obtain from the Peruvian minister to Japan, Dr. Ricardo Rivera Schreiber, information almost a year prior to the attack regarding Japan's general attack plan and targeting of Pearl Harbor. Dr. Schreiber wrote, "The Japanese military forces were planning, in the event of trouble with the Untied States, to attempt a surprise mass attack on Pearl Harbor using all their military sources." [148] Ambassador Grew sent a report via encrypted telegraph to Secretary of State Cordell Hull and to the Army Intelligence section and the Office of Naval Intelligence. Lieutenant Commander Arthur H. McCollum, director of the ONI Far East Asian section, provided the president with intelligence reports on Japan and oversaw every intercepted and decoded Japanese military and diplomatic report destined for the White House.[149] The White House directed McCollum specifically to analyze the Ambassador's cable. McCollum discounted Grew's cable as rumor and chose not to alert the Pacific Fleet that its presence at Pearl Harbor might provide Japan a high-payoff target in the event of war. He wrote in his February 1, 1941 analysis to the newly appointed commander of the Pacific Fleet, Admiral Husband E. Kimmel that "The division of the Naval Intelligence places no credence in these rumors. Furthermore, based on known data regarding the present disposition and employment of Japanese naval and army forces, no movement against Pearl Harbor appears

---

[147]Ibid., 30.

[148]Senate Committee, *Report of the Joint Committee on the Investigation of the Pearl Harbor Attack*, Executive Summary, 77; Wohlstetter, *Pearl Harbor*, 368; Prange, *At Dawn We Slept*, 30.

[149]Wohlstetter, *Pearl Harbor*, 39.

imminent or planned for the foreseeable future."[150]

Office of the Coordination of Information

As the United States entry into World War II seemed to draw closer in 1941, President Franklin Roosevelt created the country's first peacetime civilian intelligence agency, the Office of the Coordinator of Information (CIO) located in Washington D.C. He gave the CIO the responsibility of organizing the activities of several agencies to unify all of the information presented to him.[151] The president established the CIO because of the challenges associated with the Army and Navy's agreement to alternate the responsibility of providing the president with copies of the translated MAGIC message.[152] William "Wild" Donovan, who later founded the wartime Office of Strategic Services, the forerunner of the CIA, headed the CIO. The president ordered all facets of the U.S. government to provide any requested information to the COI for analysis by its civilian staff.[153]

Sources of Information and Intelligence

The American intelligence professionals did not possess specific intelligence such as the exact day and time of an attack, but they did have indications from at least one highly reliable intelligence source – MAGIC. The degree to which these warnings resulted in tactical and operational decisions, while important, do not represent an intelligence failure when reports clearly warned of a looming Japanese attack – however, the sheer volume of intelligence reports

---

[150]Prange, *At Dawn We Slept*, 31-32.

[151]Christopher Andrew, *For the President's Eyes Only: Secret Intelligence and the American Presidency from Washington to Bush* (New York: Harper Collins Publishing, 1995), 91.

[152]Clausen and Lee, *Pearl Harbor*, 45.

[153]U.S. War Department Strategic Services Unit, History Project, *War Report of the OSS* (New York: Walker Publishing Company, 1976), 5, 8; Stinnett, *Day of Deceit*, 2.

created enough conflicting information to prevent senior-level leaders from arriving at a

definitive assessement regarding the likelihood of an attack. Thus, the United States lacked a

clear assessment that demanded an upgrade to the security posture in Oahu, thereby minimizing if

not preventing the damage that would occur in the event of an attack at Pearl Harbor. In the case

of Pearl Harbor, national decision makers and military leaders had access to several important

sources of intelligence, including communications intelligence (COMINT),[154] human intelligence

(HUMINT), and other sources that allowed them to conduct information and intelligence

evaluation in order to assess and remain appraised of Japanese intentions and preparations before

the attack on Pearl Harbor.[155]

COMINT intelligence derived from the decryptions and translations of the MAGIC

intercepts served as the primary source of this type of information. Both the Army and Navy

devoted special sections to decode Japanese communications. Nevertheless, little duplication of

effort took place, and historians have unearthed no evidence of the inter-service rivalry so

common in other aspects of interwar military operations.[156] Radio intercepts provided a

secondary source of COMINT. During the 1940's, the USG obtained the majority of its COMINT

through two primary sources – naval intercepts of unencrypted message traffic, and interception

and decoding of "Magic" – Japanese diplomatic traffic.[157] By late 1940, United States code

---

[154]Department of the Army, Field Manual (FM) 2-0, *Intelligence* (Washington, D.C.: Headquarters, Department of the Army, 2004), 8-1. COMINT is the intelligence derived from foreign communications by other than the intended recipients.

[155]Ibid., 6-1. HUMINT is the collection by trained human intelligence collectors of foreign information from people and multimedia to identify elements, intentions, composition, strength, dispositions, tactics, equipment, personnel, and capabilities. It uses human sources as a tool and a variety of collection methods, both passively and actively, to gather information to satisfy the commander's intelligence requirements and cross-cue other intelligence disciplines.

[156]Wohlstetter, *Pearl Harbor*, 171.

[157]Keegan, *Intelligence in War*, 194.

breakers succeeded in breaking the Japanese the diplomatic cytological code and a portion of the

Kaigun Ango code (a series of twenty nine separate Japanese naval operational codes used for

radio contact with warships, merchant vessels, naval bases, and personnel in overseas posts, such

as naval attaches).[158] As a result the U.S. Army and Navy could read Japanese diplomatic

messages sent between Tokyo and their embassies in London, Washington, Berlin and Rome.

American experts named the Japanese code "Purple," and they called intelligence derived from

these messages "Magic." At the national level, President Roosevelt regularly received from both

the Navy and Army copies of Japanese messages decoded and translated from both the Purple

and Kaigun Ango codes.[159] These intercepts enabled American civilian and military officials to

get information from Tokyo more rapidly than the Japanese officials. According to historian

Roberta Wohlstetter "the ability to read these codes gave the United States a remarkable

advantage over the enemy…America's military and government leaders had the privilege of

seeing every day the most private communications between the Japanese government and its

ambassadors."[160]

Despite the strict secrecy and security measures practiced by the Japanese, Magic

intercepts revealed Japan's intention to target Pearl Harbor and allowed Washington to predict

Japanese diplomatic efforts. According to Clausen and Lee, as early as December 6, American

intelligence officers received four last-minute MAGIC messages that together indicated with a

high degree of certainty that the U.S. government should expect an attack on Pearl Harbor in the

near future.[161] Historian Hans Trefousse has referred to these four last-minute Magic signals the

---

[158]Stinnett, *Day of Deceit*, 21; Gudmens, *Staff Ride Handbook*, 76.

[159]Clausen and Lee, *Pearl Harbor*, 45.

[160]Wohlstetter, *Pearl Harbor*, 170.

[161]Clausen and Lee, *Pearl Harbor*, 67-70.

"pilot message," the "14-part message," the "1 o'clock, time of delivery" message, and the "final code-destruction" message.[162] These messages provided clear indications that Japan intended to end formal relations with the United States – a diplomatic rupture that would amount to an act of war against the United States.[163] Based on other correlated Magic messages and intelligence gathering efforts, Navy and Army cryptologists had clear indicators of an imminent a Japanese attack on Pearl Harbor.[164] At the 1945 congressional hearings, one agency after another confirmed the significance of these messages. All of the key players in the intelligence system – the technical staff of the SIS and Navy communications, Army and Navy Intelligence, Army and Navy Operations, the State Department, the President's advisers, and the President himself – as agreed that these messages contained the crucial tip-off signals.[165] Nevertheless, this acknowledgment did not lead to a quick and effective response to the attack.

The first two messages constituted the basis for the Wind Code. On November 19, 1941, Tokyo used the J-19 code to advise its diplomats in Washington to remain on alert for a special radio broadcast in the "case of an emergency (danger of cutting off diplomatic relations) and the cutting off of international communications. Should this happen, agents would insert a special message into the middle of the daily Japanese language shortwave broadcast."[166] This message would direct the end of all normal Japanese communications traffic, and Japanese diplomats around the world would destroy all of their secret codes, code machines and other means of secret

---

[162]Trefousse, *What Happened at Pearl Harbor?*, 19.

[163]Hopkins, *The Pacific War*, 41; Stinnett, *Day of Deceit,* 227-28.

[164]Clausen and Lee, *Pearl Harbor*, 70. Clausen and Lee argue that as early as 6 December 1941, intelligence officers received information indicating reason to expect an impending attack on Pearl Harbor.

[165]Wohlstetter, *Pearl Harbor*, 219-20.

[166]Clausen and Lee, *Pearl Harbor*, 67.

communication in preparation for war.[167]

On 1 December the Japanese sent the third message via Purple code from Tokyo to Washington, but surprisingly, U.S. personnel did not translate it until 5 December. The message gave instructions to Japanese diplomats to "discontinue the use of your code machine [Purple] and dispose of it immediately."[168] The message also included detailed instructions for taking apart the code machine, breaking the most important parts of the machine, and burning the actual Purple codes. The fourth message sent on 1 December and translated on the same day gave diplomats further instructions to assist them in destroying their codes. This message instructed Japanese diplomats to "contact the Naval Attaché in that particular embassy and to use special chemicals that the Attaché possessed to destroy the chemical."[169] The Japanese sent their final Purple code message to its diplomats in Washington on 2 December. Americans translated this message on 3 December, and issued a corrected translation on 4 December. This message directed Japanese diplomats to burn the Purple codes but gave additional guidance to retain one copy of all the special codes for future use.[170] More importantly, these messages essentially provided proof of Japanese preparation for war, and constituted convincing evidence that Japan had taken steps to prepare for an eminent declaration of war against the United States. On 3 December, the Office of Naval Operations (OPNAV) in Washington sent Admiral Kimmel two advisory messages that paraphrased the intercepts. These messages not only stressed the reliability of the source but also their importance. In short, these message, interpreted in combination, demonstrated that the Japanese military would have no means of turning back

---

[167]Stinnett, *Day of Deceit*, 181-82; Wohlstetter, *Pearl Harbor*, 49-52.

[168]Stinnett, *Day of Deceit,* 182; Clausen and Lee, *Pearl Harbor,* 68.

[169]Clausen and Lee, *Pearl Harbor*, 68.

[170]Wohlstetter, *Pearl Harbor*, 48-50, 388; Clausen and Lee, *Pearl Harbor*, 68.

should they initiate an attack, that consulates could no longer effectively communicate with Japan, and therefore the U.S. should view war with Japan imminent and inevitable.[171] The 14th Naval District (COM 14) unit at Pearl Harbor analyzed radio traffic in an effort to determine the location of Japanese ships. Although the naval radio experts could not read the content of the Japanese coded messages, they could analyze the intercepted ship call signs and determine the composition and location of the Japanese fleet on naval maps with reasonable accuracy.[172]

Before the attack on Pearl Harbor the principle intelligence organizations responsible for conducting HUMINT activities – the offices of the FBI, the State Department, and the Naval Intelligence Department – sought to determine the intent and activities of the Japanese as well.[173] The FBI relied on information derived from its agents stationed in the United States and overseas, the State Department relied on reports submitted by diplomats, including ambassadors; and Navy Intelligence relied on attaches, military observes stationed abroad, and counterintelligence personnel operating within the United States and its possessions. [174]

Compared to other methods of collection, HUMINT operations played a lesser role in predicting the Pearl Harbor attack, mainly because the United States did not engage in espionage. In Tokyo and other Japanese cities, the ever-increasing censorship of HUMINT collection from Ambassador Grew and other naval observers stationed in various high-tension areas in Thailand and Indochina meant they had to rely on covert methods to collect evidence of an imminent outbreak of war and associated naval movements. Nevertheless, diplomatic reporting – especially from Ambassador Grew stationed in Tokyo – remained an excellent source, since Grew's

---

[171]Clausen and Lee, *Pearl Harbor*, 68-70; Wohlstetter, *Pearl Harbor,* 49-52.

[172]Wohlstetter, *Pearl Harbor*, 31, 383.

[173]Prange, *At Dawn We Slept*, 80.

[174]Wohlstetter, *Pearl Harbor*, 37; Stinnett, *Day of Deceit*, 83, 95-96.

reporting showed a keen insight into Japanese intention and attitudes. His reports sent to the State Department related almost exclusively to the state of mind of the Japanese people regarding their widespread support of a potential war with the United States, largely based on their enmity towards the American people.[175] According to General Miles, head of the G2, Ambassador Grew was the "most important Source for information on Japan." Grew's 17 November telegram to the Department of State support's Miles' sentiment, since in this report he accurately predicted Japan's intention to attack. Miles supported Grew's prediction, and wrote, " I take into account the probability of the Japanese exploiting every possible tactical advantage, such as surprise and initiative."[176] Due to tight Japanese security, U.S. military attaches assigned to the embassy in Tokyo could not add any support to the assessment in Ambassadors Grew's report. Under constant surveillance, attaches could not collect information. Even though attaches continued to receive invitations to military social events, the Japanese military stopped inviting them to observe ground, air or naval demonstrations in the weeks preceding the attack.

Richard Heuer insists that proper analysis rather than additional information contributes to an accurate judgment. Moreover, failure of analysis, not failure of collection usually causes major intelligence failures.[177] Based on this view, if the United States had appropriately analyzed the information available, it might have prevented or at least reduced the damage inflicted on Pearl Harbor. Government and military officials had obtained indications for the past six weeks that Japan intended to conduct a surprise attack on Pearl Harbor. For example, on 16 October Admiral Stark, the Chief of Naval Operations (CNO) warned Admiral Kimmel, Commander in

---

[175]Wohlstetter, *Pearl Harbor*, 284.

[176]Trefousse, *What Happened at Pearl Harbor?*, 19; Wohlstetter, *Pearl Harbor*, 284.

[177]Richard J. Heuer Jr., *Psychology of Intelligence Analysis* (Washington, D.C.: Center for Intelligence, 1999), 65.

Chief U.S. Fleet (CINCUS) and the Commander in Chief, Pacific Fleet (CINCPAC) and the

Commander in Chief, Atlantic Command (CINCLANT) that Japanese attack was likely and in

view of these possibilities instructed them to take due precautions such as preparatory

deployments.[178] Four days before the attack on Pearl Harbor, Magic intercepts indicated that

Tokyo ordered Japanese diplomats to destroy most of their codes and ciphers at once and burn all

other important confidential and secret documents. These diplomatic intercepts along with

massive submarine advances on Hawaii revealed by naval intercepts signaled that war was

imminent in a matter of days to anyone paying attention.[179]

WAKING THE SLEEPING GIANT – THE ATTACK ON PEARL HARBOR

According to historian Alvin D. Coox, "the smoke had barely lifted from the blazing hulks at

Pearl Harbor on 7 December 1941, when the first American critics began to point accusing

fingers at those held responsible for the disaster in Hawaii."[180] The events surrounding the Pearl

Harbor attack remain a matter of heated debate debate today. Wohlstetter argued that the

successful Japanese attack on Pearl Harbor resulted primarily from the inability to separate the

accurate intelligence from many conflicting indicators in the period prior to the attack: "we failed

to anticipate Pearl Harbor not for want of the relevant material, but because of a plethora of

irrelevant ones," and as a result of Japan's exhaustive military preparation that including both

extensive training and detailed planning.[181] Wohlstetter went on in her book *Pearl Harbor:*

Warning and Decision to make the case that American intelligence analysts had access to too

---

[178]Wohlstetter, *Pearl Harbor*, 132.

[179]Wohlstetter, *Pearl Harbor*, 217; Stinnett, *Day of Deceit*, 182.

[180]Alvin D. Coox, "Repulsing the Pearl Harbor Revisionists: The State of Present Literature on the Debacle," *Military Affairs* 50, no. 1 (January 1986): 29.

[181]Wohlstetter, *Pearl Harbor*, 387; Toll, *Pacific Crucible, 1941-1942*, 118; Prange, *At Dawn We Slept*, 98-106.

much information, not too little, and that the nuggets indicating an imminent attack remained buried inwhat she called the "noise."[182] Separating the intelligence signals from the noise proved an extremely delicate and difficult task that exceeded the capacity of theater commanders and their intelligence sections.[183] In short, overloaded intelligence organizations simply lacked the capability to make an adequate and accurate evaluation of the information available.[184]

Japanese preparation included key military innovations that tailored the assaulting force to the specific conditions it would face. The IJN fitted its torpedoes with fins to enable them to function in the shallow waters of Pearl Harbor. It designed bombs made from large armor-piercing shells that aviation forces could drop from high-flying aircraft.[185] The Japanese military understood that it must achieve the element of surprise to enjoy success in an attack on Pearl Harbor.[186] The Japanese achieved this largely by maintaining strict radio silence as they headed eastward.[187] Once Japan attained the element of surprise, the U.S. Army personnel on Oahu could not prevent the attack – at best, they might minimize its impact by mounting an effective defense. Thus, the Army had not spent years of hard work preparing for this day totally in vain, and yet

---

[182]Wohlstetter, *Pearl Harbor,* 71-166, 228-277. Wohlstetter used the term "noise" to describe the overwhelming amount of information available to cryptologists.

[183]Wohlstetter, *Pearl Harbor, 228.*

[184]Tom Johnson, "What Every Cryptologist Should Know about Pearl Harbor," *Cryptologic Quarterly* (September 2007): 59, *Wohlstetter, Pearl Harbor, 394.*

[185]Keegan, *Intelligence in War*, 190; Spencer Tucker and Priscilla M. Roberts, *World War II: A Student Encyclopedia,* http://lumen.cgsccarl.com/login?url=http://search.ebscohost .com/login.aspc ?direct=true&db=nlebk&AN=127939&site=ehost-liveebv=1&ppid=pp_991 (accessed 28 Novemeber 2012).

[186]Tucker and Roberts, *World War II: A Student Encyclopedia.*

[187] Keegan, *Intelligence in War*, 194; New York Times, http://topics.nytimes.com/top/ reference/timestopics /subjects/w/world_war_ii_/pearl_harbor/index.html (accessed 20 January 2013).

Hawaiian Department personnel could only lessen the severity of the now-inevitable blow that Japan's surprise attack would soon deliver – and given the limitations of the department's equipment and response capability it would soon learn how vulnerable a target Pearl Harbor remained.

While military leaders on Oahu had struggled to develop plans to meet a possible Japanese attack, many Americans conceived of Hawaii as an impregnable fortress. A vast protective expanse of water shielded Oahu on all sides. Some military experts considered the great area of "vacant sea" to the north the best and most likely avenue of approach for the enemy, but these same individuals assessed that it provided an open highway of exposure and detection.[188] The Japanese would have to operate at the outer limit of their effective range in order to strike United States forces – particularly those stationed in Hawaii. Recognizing this significant factor, many Americans simply could not believe that Japan would risk an attack against American forces in the Pacific. National leaders in Washington generally believed that Japan simply did not possess the strength and natural resources to pose a serious threat to the United States. The September 1941 War Department G2 estimate of the Japanese Navy reflected this view, reporting that the Japanese military possessed no seaborne aircraft that could catch one of the new Army B-24 heavy bombers, capable of flying 290 miles per hour at an altitude of 15,000 feet.[189] At 0350 hours on 7 Dec 1941, United States Coast Guard ship Condor made the first contact of the battle less than 2 miles southwest of Pearl Harbor's entrance buoys. After receiving visual warning from the Condor at 0357 hours, destroyer USS Ward began patrolling

[188]Prange, *At Dawn We Slept*, 96.

[189]Conn, Engelman, and Fairchild, *Guarding The United States and its Outposts*, 176, 195; Zimm, *Attack On Pearl Harbor*, 38, 372-73, 378-79; Gillion, *FDR Leads The Nation Into War*, 44.

the harbor entrance. At 0637 hours, Ward sighted the periscope of a Japanese submarine.[190] Ward

attacked the area with depth charges as destroyer USS Monaghan set sail to join her in the

submarine hunt. At 0740 hours Kimmel received the information about the submarine contact,

but no report ever reached the Army.[191]

The second contact with the Japanese occurred at 7:02 a.m. when two Army radar

operators at Oahu's northern shore radar station detected the Japanese air attack approaching. The

operators contacted a junior officer who disregarded their reports, thinking the soldiers had

merely observed a group of American B-17s inbound from the U.S. West Coast. Early warning

radar was a new technology in 1941, and people could easily misinterpret it.[192] At little before 8

a.m., Japanese aircraft attacked the U.S. Pacific Fleet and associated forces at Pearl Harbor and

Oahu's military and naval facilities, with most of the ships docked and most airplanes parked in

neat rows on their airfields.[193] In two waves, coming in from the north, they proceeded to strafe,

bomb, and torpedo the fleet, the naval base, and the airfields. In two hours, they destroyed or

damaged 188 of Oahu's 394 aircraft, and sank or crippled eighteen warships.[194] At noon on 8

December, Roosevelt addressed a joint session of Congress and gave his famous speech in which

he referred to the previous day as "a day that would live in infamy." The United States had now

---

[190]Senate Committee, *Report of the Joint Committee on the Investigation of the Pearl Harbor Attack Congress of the United States*, 66.

[191]Wohlstetter, *Pearl Harbor*, 16-18.

[192]Clausen and Lee, *Pearl Harbor,*73; Senate Committee, *Report of the Joint Committee on the Investigation of the Pearl Harbor Attack*, 66, 152, 262; Senate Committee, *Hearings Before the Joint Committee on the Investigation of the Pearl Harbor Attack*, Part I, November 15-17, 19-21, and 73.

[193]For more information on the arrival of the American fleet to Hawaii, see Miller, *War Plan Orange*, 51-52.

[194]Linn, *Guardians of Empire*, 247.

entered the war that Roosevelt and many American citizens had hoped so desperately to avoid.[195]

The events of December 7, 1941 illustrated the many limitations of the island defense early warning system. While tests had proven that radars could detect incoming airplanes, they lacked the ability to distinguish between friendly and enemy.[196] This limitation significantly delayed the response because radar operators had to take extra steps to determine friend or foe based on flight schedules and projected friendly aircraft locations. Once the radar operators on duty that morning determined that they had detected enemy incoming airplanes, they telephoned the switchboard at the information center; however, the operator did not know what to do with this information because the information center was not in operation at that time.[197] The radar operators called back a few minutes later, at which time they reached Lieutenant Kermit Tyler, the pursuit officer and assistant to the controller on duty that morning. He instructed them to "forget about it," but the operators disregarded his instructions and continued to track the enemy planes as they approached Oahu.[198] The operators continued to urge Tyler to respond, but due to his inexperience he assessed it to be friendly planes coming from California therefore he never telephoned the Fourteenth Pursuit Wing.[199] According to historian Gordon Prange, "from a practical standpoint it made little difference for the pursuit officer to call the Fourteenth Pursuit Wing because due to the alert level emplaced by Short there wasn't enough time to disperse

---

[195]Hopkins, *The Pacific War*, 44.

[196]Senate Committee, *Report of the Joint Committee on the Investigation of the Pearl Harbor Attack*, Executive Summary, 141, 161; Stinnett, *Day of Deceit*, 239; Clausen and Lee, *Pearl Harbor*, 73; Prange, *At Dawn We Slept*, 500.

[197]Wohlstetter, *Pearl Harbor,* 11; Stinnett, *Day of Deceit*, 239.

[198]Prange, *At Dawn We Slept*, 500-01; Stinnett, *Day of Deceit*, 237; Wohlstetter, *Pearl Harbor,* 11-12.

[199]Wohlstetter, *Pearl Harbor,* 11; Prange, *At Dawn We Slept*, 501.

planes, distribute ammunition and elevate the alert level."[200] Time ran out for the defenders of Oahu, the attack on Pearl Harbor was well under way.

The Joint Committee investigation record disclosed that from the time the Pacific Fleet arrived at Pearl Harbor until the attack on December 7, the high command at Hawaii, both in the Army and in the Navy, frequently advised the military authorities in Washington of the shortages in the defense equipment required to safeguard Pearl Harbor.[201] Nowhere in the Joint Committee Investigation records does it appear that government authorities saw the equipment requests made by the high command in Hawaii as unreasonable or unsuitable. On the contrary, the Joint Committee acknowledged the necessity for such equipment, and could only offer budget and equipment shortages as an explanation for its denial of the Hawaiian Department's requests.[202]

CONCLUSION

Findings

Despite the fact that the attack on Pearl Harbor occurred over 70 years ago, historians continue to debate the causes of Japan's success and argue whether the attack on Pearl Harbor came as a surprise to the Untied States. According to author Zvi Lanir, surprises are inevitable;

---

[200]Prange, *At Dawn We Slept*, 501; Wohlstetter, *Pearl Harbor*, 11. The attack took place on the first Sunday morning in six weeks in which the Interceptor Command had not directed a drill for the Army Antiaircraft Artillery Corps with the Fleet Air Arm. Even if the Corps had conducted an exercise that day, it could not have responded to the incoming enemy planes because units did not use live ammunition during these exercises, and it would have taken longer to issue ammunition to the deployed guns than warning time allowed. (See General Burgins' testimony, *Hearings Before the joint Committee on the Investigation of the Pearl Harbor Attack*, Part 28, 1357).

[201]Senate Committee, *Report of the Joint Committee on the Investigation of the Pearl Harbor Attack*, Part 15, Joint Committee Exhibits No. 44 through 87; Senate Committee, *Report of the Joint Committee on the Investigation of the Pearl Harbor Attack*, Part 16, Joint Committee Exhibits No. 88 through 110.

[202]Senate Committee, *Report of the Joint Committee on the Investigation of the Pearl Harbor Attack*, 544-546.

they come from the limits of people's knowledge and understanding of their environment and themselves. Although advances in science, technology, and organizations have increased our ability to comprehend and control our environment; painful surprises remain inevitable. Lanir goes on to describe two types of surprises: fundamental and situational.[203] Situational surprises are those surprises like the one at Pearl Harbor, in which the United States took steps to prevent an incident but it happened anyway. One has a sense of self, the environment, the other (in this case the enemy or Japan), and the relations between them. "In principle one can design early warning systems to prevent surprises since surprises are related to specific events, locations, and time frames."[204]

Even though the attack on Pearl Harbor possessed an element of shock, one cannot discount the fact that the United States recognized the threat from Japan and for 20 years prepared, and took steps to prevent the incident. Simply put, the United States recognized the possibility of an attack from Japan and took step at the operational and strategic levels to prevent or mitigate the effects should such an attack take place.[205]

For more than three decades the United States refined its war plans to address the threat presented by Japan and protect its possessions in the Pacific. The United States took further steps to refine strategic war plans into the operational Joint Coastal Frontier Defense Plan and the Hawaiian Coastal Defense of Oahu. The weakness in American preparations did not revolve around planning; rather it reflected an inability to respond effectively to an attack. American strategic planners overestimated their military strength. Despite focusing on Europe as the

---

[203]Zvi Lanir, "Fundamental Surprises: The National Intelligence Crisis," *The Journal of Strategic Studies* 16, no.1 (Tel Aviv: Hakibutz HaMeuhad and Jaffe Center, 1983): 25.

[204]Ibid., 25-26.

[205]Linn, *Guardians of Empire*, 85.

priority front in this new war, planners denied the Hawaiian Department's requests for much needed equipment, personnel, and other resources, preventing Oahu defense forces from preparing to execute their planned defense quickly and effectively in the event of an attack. These plans also served as the basis for joint operating plans, mobilization plans, and a method for cooperation between the Army and Navy, to include intelligence sharing and cooperation – and in these areas planning did not adequately mesh with reality.[206]

The intelligence community failed to wholly share the intelligence that was available. Compartmentalization of intelligence meant no one organization possessed a complete threat picture. To over come this problem the intelligence community should have established an intelligence fusion cell. A fusion cell could have provided timely, relevant, and focused intelligence, threat assessments, and recommendations to defenders and discussion makers.

Many of the intelligence organizations operating in the period before the attack remained in their infancy. Nevertheless, these organizations each assessed that Japan harbored ever-growing hostile intentions towards the United States. American intelligence organizations recognized the indicators attained from a wide variety of intelligence and diplomatic sources that pointed to Pearl Harbor as a potential target.[207] However, individual agencies, by not sharing their assessments, did not provide a complete intelligence picture to the decision makers who needed it. This did not result from negligence, but because of the compartmentalization of information and other policies that limited intelligence collection and sharing. Again, no function or organization existed to fuse intelligence between the Navy and Army or provide holistic

---

[206]Senate Committee, *Report of the Joint Committee on the Investigation of the Pearl Harbor Attack*, Navy Court of Inquiry Exhibits No. 4 and 5, Part 15, , 82–83.

[207]Parker, *Pearl Harbor Revisited*, 26; Ross, *U.S. War Plans 1938-1945*, 2. Throughout the 1930s, Joint Board war planners consistently found an attack against Pearl Harbor far more likely than one against the mainland.

assessments to government officials. Consequently, the intelligence organization could not set

intelligence priorities or focus their collection efforts. This lack of centralized command, control,

and coordination between the intelligence organizations affected the ability for the defenders of

Oahu to take effective action against an attack because an inadequate sense of urgency existed

among the forces stationed on Oahu, who remained desensitized and unprepared well beyond the

point that observers knew an attack was imminent.

Historians Cohen and Gooch stated that " a vigorous defense of Oahu was entirely

possible, one critical failure was that of alertness of the active defenses….the ability to come into

play within minutes, or perhaps as much as a half an hour of warning."[208] Even though the

defenders of Pearl Harbor relied heavily on the newly developed radar system to provide early

warning and detection of incoming long-range objects, radar systems had served as a major factor

in the British victory during the Battle of Britain, and independent British and American tests

upheld the efficacy of the systems.[209] As a result, planners expected radar systems to provide

timely early warning thereby allowing an appropriate response while enemy attackers remained at

a safe distance.

In reality, the air defense and radar systems in Oahu as established proved inadequate to

provide early warning against any potential attacks, and planners should have understood this

before the morning of the attack. Because the operation center operated for limited hours, and

lacked a reliable mode of communications with the information center, radars provided

inadequate warning given ground forces' response times. Even though radars could detect

---

[208]Cohen and Gooch, *Military Misfortunes*, 50.

[209]Butowsky, "Early Warnings": 4. In 1935, radars played a major role in winning the Battle of Britain, and in 1940 England and the United States began collaborating in the further development and refinement of radar technology. When American forces tested the radar system in Waianae and Koko Head, they successfully detected planes at a range of 85 miles from the coast.

incoming airplanes, they lacked the ability to distinguish between friendly and enemy planes.[210]

In addition, the defenders of Oahu lacked all the necessary equipment required to carry out the

defense plan, and integration of the AWC and AIC commands and mission into a combined and

well-functioning unit had not occurred.[211] In addition, Hawaiian Department personnel had not

fully integrated radar into Oahu's air defense system. While the radar functioned as intended and

detected the incoming Japanese planes, no ability existed to assess this information and

communicating reliable intelligence to those in command. As a result, the Army high command

did not learn about the radar sighting at Opana until after the attack – but even if they had,

temporal and physical limitations in the Army's ability to respond meant that aircraft would

remain on the ground and coastal defense systems would remain unmanned until well after the

attack commenced.[212]

Implications

Revisiting the historical debate regarding the cause of Japan's success in its 1941 attack

against Pearl Harbor offers insight for today's homeland defense planners hoping to prevent

another attack on U.S. soil like the one conducted by Al Qaeda on September 11, 2001. For

example, Hurricane Katrina occurred in 2005, just five years after the attacks of 9/11, three years

after the establishment of the Department of Homeland Security (DHS) and one year after DHS

developed a National Response Plan. Despite this intense focus on homeland security, most

analysts judge the response to Katrina a failure. Like in the case of Pearl Harbor, many

government officials seemed surprised by the delayed response and poor reaction by many of

---

[210]Senate Committee, *Report of the Joint Committee on the Investigation of the Pearl Harbor Attack*, Executive Summary , 141, 161; Stinnett, *Day of Deceit*, 239; Clausen and Lee, *Pearl Harbor*, 73; Prange, *At Dawn We Slept*, 500.

[211]Butowsky. "Early Warnings": 4.

[212]Ibid., 5.

those tasked to respond. The titles of two congressional reports highlight this sense of failure. In 2006, a Select House Committee issued a report on the Katrina response entitled "A Failure of Initiative." That same year, the Senate Committee on Homeland Security and Governmental Affairs prepared a report entitled "A Nation Still Unprepared." These reports emphasized the continued shortcomings in America's homeland defense and response capability.[213]

The source of this failure did not center on a single event or factor; rather, it stemmed from an accumulation of failures through both action and inaction. The executive summary of the report referred to "failures" on the part of government in responding to Katrina. The committee found that many of these failures resulted from poor information flow and a lack of initiative on the part of government. The committee report includes an extensive list of the failures it identified. These include a lack of warning systems, failure of the federal government to develop a coordinated plan to meet the disaster, communications problems, lack of situational awareness, and poor command and control leading to the absence of unity of command.[214] Much like the organizations responsible for the defense of Oahu and Pearl Harbor, responders failed to convert information into a level of preparation appropriate with the scope of the impending disaster. The dispersed nature of authority in the U.S. intergovernmental system led to further inertia as federal responders failed to recognize the need to engage more quickly and effectively.[215]

Sixty years after the attack on Pearl Harbor, the United States still does not appear to see the similarities between events like Katrina and the Japanese attack on Pearl Harbor or learn from

---

[213]Donald P. Moynihan, *From Forest Fires to Hurricane Katrina: Case Studies of Incident Command System.* Report to the IBM Center for the Business of Government, 2007, 1.

[214]House Committee, *A Failure of Initiative: Final Report of the Select Bipartisan Committee to Investigate the Preparation for and Response to Katrina,* 109th Cong., 2d sess., 2006, Rep. 000-000, 183-84.

[215]Donald P. Moynihan, *From Forest Fires to Hurricane Katrina: Case Studies of Incident Command System.* Report to the IBM Center for the Business of Government, 2007, 1.

the valuable lessons of that incident. Irrespective of intelligence or early warning capabilities and organizations, only effective intelligence and operations fusion can ensure that the United States develops the ability to coordinate and synchronize activities in such a manner than it can respond effectively to a threat to the homeland. The lack of such intelligence fusion capability leaves the nation at risk – whether to another military attack like Pearl Harbor, or a wholly different sort of threat like Hurricane Katrina or one of the many possible scenarios currently envisioned involving a terrorist attack against the homeland.

BIBLIOGRAPHY

Ameringer, Charles D. *U.S. Foreign Intelligence: The Secret Side of American History.* Lexington: Lexington Books, 1990.

Andrew, Christopher. *For the Presidents Eyes Only: Secret Intelligence and the American Presidency from Washington to Bush.* New York: Harper Collins Publishing, 1995.

Ball, Harry P. *Of Responsible Command: A History of the U.S. Army War College the School that Shaped the Military Leaders of the Free World.* Carlisle Barracks: Alumni Association of the United States Army, 1994.

Bernstein, Richard. On Dec. 7, "Did We Know We Knew?" (15 December1999) http://topics.nytimes.com/top/reference/timestopics/subjects/w/world_war_ii_/pearl_harb or/index.html. (accessed 20 January 2013).

Budge, Kent G. Pearl Harbor, "The Pacific War Online Encyclopedia, 2007" http://pwencycl.kgbudge.com/P/e?Pearl_Harbor.htm (accessed 28 January 2013).

Butowsky, Harry A. "Early Warnings: The Mystery of Radar in Hawaii." *Cultural Resources Management* 23, no. 3 (January 1999): 4-7.

Calhoun, Mark T. "Lesley J. McNair: Little-Known Architect of the U.S. Army." Lecture, University of Kansas Hall Center, Lawrence, March 4, 2011.

Clausen, Henry C. and Lee Bruce. *Pearl Harbor: Final Judgment.* New York: Crown Publishers, Inc., 1992.

Cohen, Eliot A. and Gooch, John. *Military Misfortunes The Anatomy of Failure in War.* New York: Vintage Books, 1990.

Conn, Stetson, Engelman, Rose C., and Fairchild, Byron. *Guarding The United States and Its Outposts.* Washington D.C.: U.S. Government Printing Office, 2000.

Coox, Alvin D. "Repulsing the Pearl Harbor Revisionists: The State of Present Literature on the Debacle," *Military Affairs* 50, no. 1 (January 1986): 29.

Department of the Army. Army Doctrine Publication (ADP) 3-0, *Unified Land Operations.* Washington, DC: Headquarters, Department of the Army, 2011.

Department of the Army. U.S. Army Field Manual (FM) 2-0, *Intelligence.* Washington, D.C.: Headquarters, Department of the Army, 2004.

Doenecke, Justus D. and Wilz, John E. *From Isolation to War, 1931-1941.* Arlington Heights: Harlan Davidson Inc., 1991.

Freeman, Richard. *Pearl Harbor: Hinge of War.* Chicago: University of Chicago Press, 2007.

Gillion, Steven M. *FDR Leads the Nation Into War.* New York: Basic Books, 2011.

Gole, Henry G. *The Road to Rainbow: Army Planning for Global War, 1934-1940.* Annapolis: Naval Institute Press, 2003.

———. "War Planning at the War College in the Mid-1930s." *Parameters, Journal of the U.S. Army War College* (1984): 52-64.

Goralski, Robert, and Russell W. Freeburg. Oil and War: *How the Deadly Struggle for Fuel in WWI Meant Victory or Defeat.* New York: William Morrow and Co., 1987.

Gudmens, Jeffrey J. *Staff Ride Handbook for the Attack on Pearl Harbor, 7 December 1941: A Study of Defending America.* Fort Leavenworth: Combat Studies Institute Press, 2009.

Greenfield, Kent R., ed. *The War Against Japan, U.S. Army in World War II Pictorial Record.* Washington D.C.: Government Printing Office, 2001.

Herring, George C. *From Colony to Superpower: U.S. Foreign Relations Since 1776.* Oxford: Oxford University Press, 2008.

Heuer, Richard J. Jr., *Psychology of Intelligence Analysis.* Washington, D.C.: Center for Intelligence, 1999.

Hopkins, William B. *The Pacific War: The Strategy, Politics, and Players That Won The War.* Minneapolis: Zenith Press, 2008.

Hanyok, Robert J. "How the Japanese Did It." Naval History Magazine 23, no. 6, (December 2009). http://www.usni.org/magazines/navalhistory/2009-12/how-japanese-did-it (accessed 28 January 2013).

Johnson, Tom "What Every Cryptologist Should Know about Pearl Harbor," *Cryptologic Quarterly* (September 2007): 59.

Kahn, David. *The Code Breakers: The Comprehensive History of Secret Communications from Ancient Times to the Internet.* New York: Scribner Book Co., 1996.

Keegan, John. *Intelligence in War: The Value and Limitations of What the Military Can Learn About the Enemy.* New York: Vintage Books, 2002.

Lanir, Zvi. "Fundamental Surprises: The National Intelligence Crisis: *The Journal of Strategic Studies* 16, no.1. Tel Aviv: Hakibutz HaMeuhad and Jaffe Center, (1983).

Linn, Brian M. *Guardians of Empire, the U.S. Army and the Pacific, 1902-1940.* Chapel Hill: University of North Carolina Press, 1997.

Levite, Ariel. *Intelligence and Strategic Surprises.* New York: Colombia University Press, 1987.

Mawdsley, Evan. "Countdown to Global War, Part Three." http://www.yalebooks. worldpress.com (accessed 26 November 2011).

McFarlane, Munroe. "Analysis and Discussion", *Map Problem No. 30, Part 3-Problems and Exercises*, vol. 55, CAWC 1914-15, Box 5, AWCIR.

Miller, Edward S. *War Plan Orange The U.S. Strategy to Defeat Japan, 1897 - 1945.* Annapolis: Naval Institute Press, 1991.

Millet, Allan R. and Peter Maslowski. *For the Common Defense a Military History of the United States of America.* New York: The Free Press, 1994.

Moynihan, Donald P. From Forest Fires to Hurricane Katrina: Case Studies of Incident Command Systems. Report to the IBM Center for the Business of Government, 2007.

Parker, Fredrick D. *Pearl Harbor Revisited: United States Navy Communications Intelligence 1924-1942, Series IV - World War II, Volume 6.* Fort Meade: National Security Agency, 1994.

Piacine, Robert F. "Pearl Harbor: Failure of Intelligence." Master's thesis, Maxwell Air Force Base: Air War College, 1997.

Prange, Gordon W. and Donald Goldstein M. *At Dawn We Slept: The Untold Story of Pearl Harbor.* New York: Penguin Books Ltd., 1981.

Record, Jeffery. "Japan's Decision for War in 1941: Some Enduring Lessons." Master's thesis, U.S. Army War College, 2009.

Ross, Steven T. *U.S. War Plans 1938-1945*. Boulder: Lynne Rienner Publisher, Inc., 2002.

Spector, Ronald H. *Eagle Against the Sun: The American War with Japan*. New York: The Free Press, 1984.

Stinnett, Robert B. *Day of Deceit: The Truth About FDR and Pearl Harbor*. New York: The Free Press, 2000.

Toll, Ian W. *Pacific Crucible War at Sea in the Pacific, 1941-1942*. New York: W.W. Norton & Company, 2012.

Trefousse, Hans L. *What Happened at Pearl Harbor? Documents Pertaining to the Japanese Attack of December 7, 1941, and Its Background*. New York: Twayne Publisher, 1958.

Tucker, Spencer and Priscilla M. Roberts, "World War II: A Student Encyclopedia," http://lumen.cgsccarl.com/login?url= http://search.ebscohost.com/login.aspc?direct= true&db=nlebk&AN=127939&site=ehost-liveebv=1&ppid=pp_991 (accessed March 15, 2013).

U.S. Army Center of Military History. *A Brief History of the U.S. Army in World War II*. Washington D.C.: Government Printing Office, 1992.

U.S. Congress, House. *A Failure of Initiative: Final Report of the Select Bipartisan Committee to Investigate the Preparation for and Response to Katrina*. 109th Cong., 2nd sess., 2006. Report 000-000.

U.S. Congress, Senate. *Hearings Before the Joint Committee on the Investigation of the Pearl Harbor Attack*, 39 vols. 79th Cong., 1st sess., 1946.

———. *Hurricane Katrina: A Nation Still Unprepared: Special Report of the Committee on Homeland Security and Governmental Affairs*. 109th Cong., 2nd sess., 2006. Special Report 109-322.

———. *Report of the Joint Committee on the Investigation of the Pearl Harbor Attack*. 79th Cong., 2nd sess., 1946. Document No. 244.

U.S. War Department Strategic Services Unit, History Project. *War Report of the OSS*. New York: Walker Publishing Company, 1976.

Vandiver, Frank. *1001 Things Everyone Should Know About World War II*. New York: Random House Inc., 2002.

Watson, Mark. *The War Department Chief of Staff: Prewar Plans and Preparations*. The United States Army in World War II. Washington D.C.: United States Army Center of Military History, 1991.

Wilson, Sandra. *The Manchurian Crisis and Japanese Society, 1931-33*. London: Routledge Press, 2002.

Wohlstetter, Roberta. *Pearl Harbor Warning and Decision*. Stanford: Stanford University Press, 1962.

Woodbridge, Bingham, Hilary Conroy, and Frank W. Ikle. *A History of Asia Vol. II*. Boston: Allyn and Bacon, 1965.

Zimm, Alan. *Attack on Pearl Harbor: Strategy, Combat, Myths, and Deceptions*. Havertown: Casemate Publishers, 2011.